LANGUAGE *of* MATHEMATICS

For Class IX & X

LANGUAGE *of* MATHEMATICS

For Class IX & X

(As per Latest CBSE Syllabus)

Er. PREM KUMAR
B.E., M.Sc.

EPH®
Eurasia Publishing House

EURASIA PUBLISHING HOUSE
(An imprint of S Chand Publishing)
A Division of S Chand And Company Limited
(An ISO 9001 Certified Company)
Head Office : D-92, Sector 2, Noida, Uttar Pradesh-201 301
Phone : 0120-468 2700, **e-mail :** info@schandpublishing.com
Registered Office : A-27, 2nd Floor, Mohan Co-operative Industrial Estate, New Delhi–110 044
www.schandpublishing.com;
e-mail : helpdesk@schandpublishing.com

Marketing Offices :

Chennai	:	Ph: 044-2363 2120, chennai@schandpublishing.com
Guwahati	:	Ph: 0361-406 6369, guwahati@schandpublishing.com
Hyderabad	:	Ph: 040-4018 6018, hyderabad@schandpublishing.com
Jalandhar	:	Ph: 0181-464 5630, jalandhar@schandpublishing.com
Kolkata	:	Ph: 033-2335 7458, kolkata@schandpublishing.com
Lucknow	:	Ph: 0522-400 3633, lucknow@schandpublishing.com
Mumbai	:	Ph: 022-2500 0297, mumbai@schandpublishing.com
Patna	:	Ph: 0612-226 0011, patna@schandpublishing.com

First Published in 2011
Revised Edition 2012
Reprints 2011, 2013, 2014, 2017, 2018 (Twice), 2021, 2022, 2023, 2025

ISBN : 978-81-21936-39-2 **Product Code :** SCS3LOM102MATAB17MLN

PRINTED IN INDIA
By Vikas Publishing House Private Limited, Plot 20/4, Site-IV, Industrial Area Sahibabad, Ghaziabad–201 010 and Published by S Chand And Company Limited, A-27, 2nd Floor, Mohan Co-operative Industrial Estate, New Delhi–110 044.

PREFACE

LANGUAGE OF MATHEMATICS for Class IX and X has been written in accordance with the latest CBSE syllabus. This book not only provides definitions and formulae but also explains the concepts with easy to understand language.

As a teacher, I have felt the need for such a book for a long time. Many of my students urged me to take up this project. I thank them for their inspiration, and their faith in me. I also gratefully acknowledge the help of S. CHAND & COMPANY LTD. who did all they could to give the book the best possible form. I look forward to suggestions from readers for the improvement the book.

I am thankful to the Management Team and the Editorial Department of S. Chand & Company Ltd. for all help and support in the publication of this book for class IX and X.

I also convey our sincere thanks to our family for their kind co-operation and valuable support during the writing of this book.

Although every effort has made to keep this book error free, still some printing errors might have crept in. If you notice any mistake, error or discrepancy, I would be extremely thankful if the same are brought to my notice. You may send in your valuable suggestions, feedback or queries by post or through email to **mathspoint9818159014@gmail.com** or feel free to at 9818159014.

Er. PREM KUMAR

Maths Point
E-19/293, Sector – 3
Rohini, Delhi- 110085

PREFACE

LAXMI'S DREAM MATHEMATICS for Class IX and X has been written in accordance with the latest CBSE syllabus. This book not only provides definitions and formulae but also explains the concepts with easy to understand language.

As a teacher, I have felt the need for such a book for a long time. Many of my students urged me to take up this project. I thank them for their inspiration, and their faith in me. I also gratefully acknowledge the help of S. CHAND & COMPANY LTD. who did all they could to give the book the best possible form. I look forward to suggestions from readers for the improvement of the book.

I am thankful to the Management Team and the Editorial Department of S. Chand & Company Ltd. for all help and support in the publication of this book for Class IX and X.

I also convey my sincere thanks to my family for their kind co-operation and valuable support during the writing of this book.

Although every effort has been made to keep this book error free, still some printing errors might have crept in. If you notice any mistake, error or discrepancy, I would be extremely thankful if the same are brought to my notice. You may send in your valuable suggestions, feedback or queries by post or through email to [illegible] or feel free to call 9818151014

Dr. [illegible] LAXMI [illegible]

Maths Point
B-1/9/23, Sector 15
Rohini, Delhi-110085

CONTENTS

Symbols

=	:	is equal to
≠	:	is not equal to
:	:	is to
::	:	is as
∴	:	therefore, hence
∵	:	since
±	:	plus or minus
≅	:	congruent to
≡	:	identically equal to
>	:	greater than
<	:	less than
∞	:	infinity
Σ	:	sigma
α	:	is proportional to (or) varies as
∈	:	belongs to
∉	:	does not belong to
{ }	:	set
{ϕ}	:	empty set
⇒	:	implies
⇔	:	implies and implied by
↔	:	equivalent
→	:	ray
—	:	line segment
⊥	:	is perpendicular to
∥	:	is parallel to
Δ	:	triangle
▭	:	rectangle
□	:	square
○	:	circle
$\bigcirc_{ce}$	:	Circumference
°	:	degree

π (pi)	:	, $\frac{22}{7}$
$\sqrt{\ }$	:	**square root**
$\sqrt[n]{\ }$	:	**nth root of**
( )	:	**small bracket (Parenthesis)**
[ ]	:	**square bracket**
{ }	:	**flower bracket (or braces)**
∀	:	**for all**
N	:	**Natural numbers**
W	:	**Whole numbers**
Z	:	**Integers**
R	:	**Real numbers**

FOR CLASS – IX

CHAPTER 1

NUMBER SYSTEMS

"Numbers Rules the Universe" : Pythagoras

Introduction

We have learnt about the various types of numbers and their representation on the number line. These are summarized below:

S.No.	Type of Number	Symbol	Definiton	Examples
1.	Natural Numbers	N	Counting numbers are known as natural numbers.	1, 2, 3, ...
2.	Whole Numbers	W	All natural numbers together with 0 form whole numbers.	0, 1, 2, 3, ...
3.	Integers	Z	All natural numbers, 0 and the negatives of natural numbers form the collection of integers.	-4, -3, -2, -1, 0, 1, 2, 3, ... [All natural numbers and whole numbers are integers.]
4.	Rational Numbers	Q	The numbers of the form $\frac{p}{q}$ where p and q are integers and $q \neq 0$ are known as rational numbers	Decimal representation is terminating or non-terminating but repeating. 0, all natural numbers, all integers, $\frac{3}{5}, -\frac{2}{7}$, ...
5.	Irrational Numbers	I	The numbers which cannot be expressed in the form $\frac{p}{q}$ where p and q are integers and $q \neq 0$ are known as irrational numbers	Decimal representation is non-terminating and non -repeating. $\pi, \sqrt{2}, \sqrt{3}$, 1.010010001... etc.

Number Line:

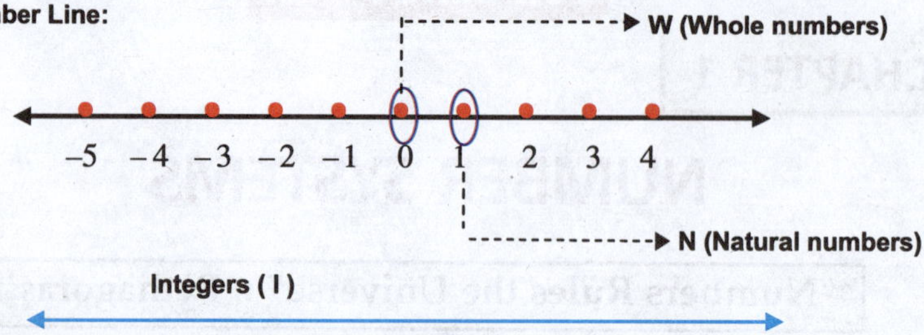

Odd number

A number which is not divisible by 2 is called an odd number.

Example: 1, 3, 5, 7, 9 ....

Even number

A number which is divisible by 2 is called an even number

Example: 2, 4, 6, 8,........................

Prime Number

Natural Number which is divisible by itself and unity is called a prime number or, prime number is a number that cannot be separated into any integral factors other than itself and 1.

Example: 2, 3, 5, 7, 11, 13, 17, 19, 23, 29, 31, 37, 41, 43, 47, ...

Real Number

The complete set of rational and irrational number is the set of real numbers and is denoted by R.

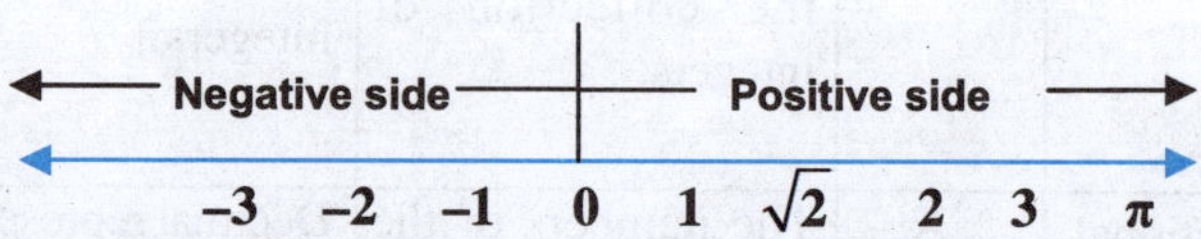

Real number can be represented as points of a line. This line is called as real line or number line.

Absolute value of Real number

There is a point on number line ***l*** which corresponds to the number x. The distance of this point x from the point **0** (zero) is called the **absolute value of *x*.**

The **absolute value** of number positive or negative is always non-negative**.** The **absolute value** of number **is written as |** x **|**. It is defined as

If $x \geq 0$ then $|x| = x$

If $x < 0$ then $|x| = -x$

Composite Number

Composite numbers are the numbers which have other divisors besides 1 and the number itself.

Example: 4, 6, 8, 9, 10, 12, 14, 15, ...

Co-prime Number

Two natural numbers (not necessarily prime) are co-prime, if their H.C.F. (Highest common factor) is one.

Example: (1, 2), (1, 3), (3, 4), (3, 10), (3, 8), (5, 6), etc.

Locating Irrational numbers on the numbers on the number line:

1. Locating $\sqrt{2}$:

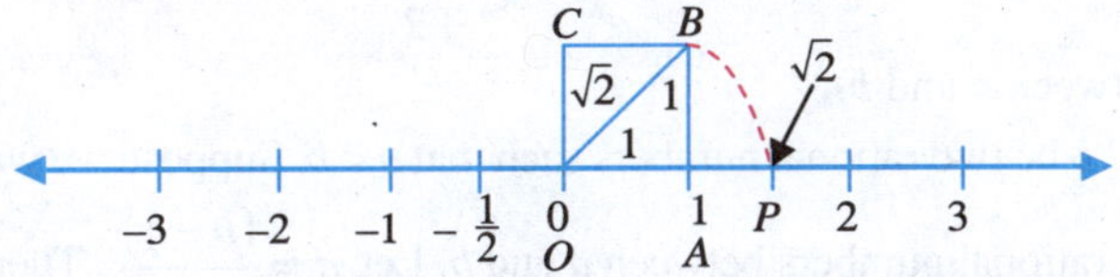

(*a*) Draw a number line and mark a point *O*, representing zero, on it.

(*b*) Let point *A* represent 1. Then, *OA* = 1

(*c*) Draw a right triangle *OAB* such that *AB* = *OA* =1.

(*d*) By Pythagoras theorem, $OB^2 = OA^2 + AB^2$

$\Rightarrow \quad OB^2 = 1^2 + 1^2 \quad \Rightarrow \quad OB = \sqrt{2}$.

(*e*) Draw a circle with centre *O* and radius *OB* which cuts the number line at P_1. Then, $OP = OB = \sqrt{2}$ ·

2. Locating $\sqrt{3}$:

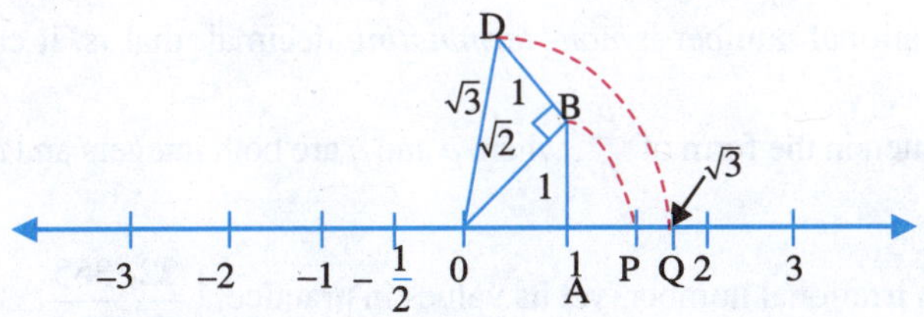

Point (a) to (d) from (1).

(*e*) Construct *BD* of unit length and perpendicular to *OB*.

(*f*) By Pythagoras theorem, $OD^2 = OB^2 + BD^2 \Rightarrow \quad OD^2 = \left(\sqrt{2}\right)^2 + 1^2$ ·

$\Rightarrow OD^2 = 3 \Rightarrow OD = \sqrt{3}$ ·

(*g*) With centre *O* and radius *OD*, draw an arc which intersects the number line at *Q*. Then $OQ = \sqrt{3}$.

POINTS TO REMEMBER

(1) A rational number $\frac{p}{q}$ is said to be in the simplest form if the integers p and q have no common factor other than 1.

(2) If $\frac{p}{q}$ is a rational number and m is non- zero integer then

$\frac{p}{q} = \frac{p \times m}{q \times m}$, so $\frac{p}{q}$ and $\frac{p \times m}{q \times m}$ are known as **equivalent rational numbers.**

(3) If a and b be two rational numbers then, $\frac{(a+b)}{2}$ is a rational number lying between a and b.

(4) Let a and b be two rational numbers such that $a < b$. Suppose we want to find n rational numbers between a and b. Let $d = \frac{(b-a)}{n+1}$. Then n rational numbers lying between a and b are:

$a + d, a + 2d, a + 3d, ..., a + nd$

(5) Every rational number can be expressed in decimal form.

(6) $\frac{p}{0}$ is not a rational number, where p is any integer.

(7) There are infinitely many rational numbers between two given rational numbers.

(8) A rational number is either terminating or non-terminating but recurring decimal.

(9) An irrational number is *non- terminating* decimal, that is, it cannot be written in the form of $\frac{p}{q}$, where p and q are both integers and $q \neq 0$.

(10) π is an irrational number, yet its values in practice $\left(\frac{22}{7}, \frac{355}{113}, 3.14\right)$ appear to be rational number. These are its **approximate** values.

(11) Sum or difference of rational number and irrational number is always irrational number.

(12) Product or quotient of a rational number (non-zero) and an irrational number is also an irrational number.

(13) Sum, difference, Product, or quotient of two irrational numbers need not be irrational.

(14) The positive *n*th root of a, i.e, $\sqrt[n]{a}$ is called a **surd** or a **radical**.

(15) Every rational number is not a surd.

(16) Every irrational number is a surd.

(17) The process of converting a surd to a rational number by multiplying it with a suitable factor, is called the rationalization of the surd.

(18) The binomial surds which differ only in sign (+ or –) between the terms connecting them, are called conjugate surds. $a+\sqrt{b}$ and $a-\sqrt{b}$ are the conjugate surds.

Decimal Representation of Rational numbers

Every rational number can be represented either as a terminating decimal or a non- terminating decimal but repeating (recurring or periodic) decimal.

$\frac{15}{8}$

```
    1.875
 8 )15
    8
   ---
    70
    64
   ---
    60
    56
   ---
    40
    40
   ---
     0
```

TERMINATING

$\frac{15}{8} = 1.875$

Non-terminating but repeating decimal

NON-TERMINATING RECURRING

$\frac{2}{3} =$ **0.666.....**

$\frac{11}{7} =$ **1.571428.....**

```
    0.666
 3 )20
    18
   ---
     20
     18
    ---
      20
      18
     ---
       2
```

```
    1.571428...
 7 ) 11
      7
    ---
     40
     35
    ---
      50
      49
     ---
       10
        7
      ---
        30
        28
       ---
         20
         14
        ---
          60
          56
         ---
           4
```

Laws of indices:

1. $a^m \times a^n = a^{m+n}$
2. $\dfrac{a^m}{a^n} = a^{m-n}$
3. $(a^m)^n = a^{m \times n}$
4. $a^0 = 1$ for all $a \neq 0$
5. $a^{-m} = \dfrac{1}{a^m}$
6. $a^{\frac{m}{n}} = \sqrt[n]{a^m}$
7. $a^m . b^m = (ab)^m$
8. $(a . b)^n = a^n . b^n$
9. $a^{\frac{1}{n}} = \sqrt[n]{a}$
10. $\left(\sqrt[n]{a}\right)^n = \left(a^{1/n}\right)^n = a$
11. $\dfrac{\sqrt[n]{a}}{\sqrt[n]{b}} = \sqrt[n]{\dfrac{a}{b}}$

Some Important results:

1. $\sqrt{a} \times \sqrt{a} = a \Rightarrow \sqrt{5} \times \sqrt{5} = 5$
2. $\sqrt{a} \times \sqrt{b} = \sqrt{ab} \Rightarrow \sqrt{3} \times \sqrt{5} = \sqrt{15}$
3. $\sqrt{a^2 b} = a\sqrt{b} = \sqrt{5^2 \times 3} = 5\sqrt{3}$
4. $\left(\sqrt{a} + \sqrt{b}\right)^2 = a + b + 2\sqrt{ab} \Rightarrow \left(\sqrt{3} + \sqrt{2}\right)^2 = 3 + 2 + 2\sqrt{6}$
5. $\left(\sqrt{a} - \sqrt{b}\right)^2 = a + b - 2\sqrt{ab} \Rightarrow \left(\sqrt{3} - \sqrt{2}\right)^2 = 3 + 2 - 2\sqrt{6}$
6. $\left(\sqrt{a} - \sqrt{b}\right)\left(\sqrt{a} + \sqrt{b}\right) = \text{a} - \text{b} \Rightarrow \left(\sqrt{3} - \sqrt{2}\right)\left(\sqrt{3} + \sqrt{2}\right) = 3 - 2$
7. $\left(\sqrt{a} + \dfrac{1}{\sqrt{a}}\right)^2 = a + \dfrac{1}{a} + 2$
8. $a^2 + \dfrac{1}{a^2} = \left(a + \dfrac{1}{a}\right)^2 - 2$
9. $a^2 + \dfrac{1}{a^2} = \left(a + \dfrac{1}{a}\right)^2 - 2$

CHAPTER 2

POLYNOMIALS

Some algebraic expressions and identities:

1. $(x+y)^2 = x^2+2xy+y^2 = (x-y)^2+4xy$
2. $(x-y)^2 = x^2-2xy+y^2 = (x+y)^2-4xy$
3. $x^2-y^2=(x-y)(x+y)$
4. $x^4-y^4=(x+y)(x-y)(x^2+y^2)$
5. $x^2+y^2=(x+y)^2-2xy = (x-y)^2+2xy$
6. $(x+y+z)^2 = x^2+y^2+z^2+2xy+2yz+2zx$
7. $x^3+y^3=(x+y)\left(x^2-xy+y^2\right) = (x+y)^3-3xy\,(x+y)$
8. $x^3-y^3=(x-y)\left(x^2+xy+y^2\right)= (x-y)^3+3xy\,(x-y)$
9. $x^3+y^3+z^3-3xyz=(x+y+z)\left(x^2+y^2+z^2-xy-yz-zx\right)$

   $=\frac{1}{2}(x+y+z)\left[(x-y)^2+(y-z)^2+(z-x)^2\right]$
10. If $x+y+z=0$, then $x^3+y^3+z^3=3xyz$
11. $x^3+y^3+z^3=(x+y+z)^3-3(x+y)(y+z)(z+x)$
12. $(x+y)^3=x^3+3x^2y+3xy^2+y^3 = x^3+y^3+3xy(x+y)$
13. $(x-y)^3=x^3-3x^2y+3xy^2-y^3 = x^3-y^3-3xy\,(x-y)$
14. $(x+a)(x+b)=x^2+(a+b)x+ab$
15. $2(x^2+y^2)=(x+y)^2+(x-y)^2$
16. $(x+y)^2-(x-y)^2=4xy$
17. $xy=\frac{1}{4}[(x+y)^2-(x-y)^2]$
18. $x^4+x^2y^2+y^4=(x^2+xy+y^2)(x^2-xy+y^2)$
19. $x^2+y^2+z^2-xy-yz-zx=0$

    $\frac{1}{2}[(x-y)^2+(y-z)^2+(z-x)^2]=0 \quad\Rightarrow x=y=z$

Remainder Theorem:

Let $p(x)$ be any polynomial of degree greater than or equal to one, and a be any real number. If $p(x)$ is divided by $(x - a)$, then the remainder is equal to $p(a)$.

(*a*) If a polynomial is divided by $(x+a)$, the remainder is given by p /(–*a*)..

$[\because\ x + a = 0 \Rightarrow x = -a]$

(*b*) If a polynomial is divided by $(ax - b)$, the remainder is given by $p\left(\frac{b}{a}\right)$.

$\left[\because ax - b = 0 \Rightarrow x = \frac{b}{a}\right]$

(*c*) If a polynomial is divided by $(ax + b)$, the remainder is given by $p\left(-\frac{b}{a}\right)$.

$\left[\because ax + b = 0 \Rightarrow x = -\frac{b}{a}\right]$

(*d*) If a polynomial is divided by $(b - ax)$, the remainder is given by $p\left(\frac{b}{a}\right)$.

$\left[\because b - ax = 0 \Rightarrow x = \frac{b}{a}\right]$

Factor Theorem:

Let $p(x)$ be any polynomial of degree greater than or equal to one and a be any real number such that $p(a) = 0$, then $(x - a)$ is a factor of $p(x)$. Conversely, if $(x - a)$ is a factor of $p(x)$, then $p(a) = 0$. Each term of a polynomial has a coefficient.

The constant polynomial 0 is called the zero polynomial. In fact, 2, -5, 7, etc. are examples of constant polynomials.

The highest power of the variable in a polynomial is called the degree of the polynomial.

The degree of a non-zero constant polynomial is zero.

A polynomial in one variable x of degree n is an expression of the form $a_nx^n + a_{n-1}x^{n-1} + \cdots + a_1x + a_0$, where $a_0, a_1, a_2, ..., a_n$ are constants and $a_n \neq 0$.

If all the constant are zero, i.e., if $a_0 = a_1 = a_2 = ... = a_n = 0$, we get the zero polynomial, which is denoted by 0. The degree of the zero polynomial is not defined.

A zero of a polynomial $p(x)$ is a number c such that $p(c) = 0$.

A non-zero constant polynomial has no zero. Every real number is a zero of the zero polynomial.

POINTS TO REMEMBER

1. **Polynomial:-** A function $p(x)$ of the form :

$$p(x) = a_0 + a_1x + a_2x^2 + ... + a_nx^n$$

where $a_0, a_1, a_2, ..., a_n$ are real numbers, $a_n \neq 0$, and n is non-negative integer, is called a "polynomial in x over real"

2. **Monomial :-** A polynomial having only one term is called a monomial. Mono means one (single). For example, 2, $3x$, $7x^2$ are monomial.
3. **Binomial :-** A polynomial having two terms is called a binomial. Bi stands for two. **Example,** $px^2 + q$
4. **Trinomial :-** A polynomial having three terms is called a trinomial. Tri means three. **Example,** $ax^2 + bx + c$
5. **Zero Polynomial :-** The polynomial having all the coefficients as zero is called a zero polynomial.

   For example, $0x^3 + 0x^2 - 0x + 0, 0y^2 + 0y + 0$

6. **Zero of a polynomial :-** The values of the variable x for which the given polynomial $p(x)$ vanishes are called zero of the polynomial.
7. **Degree of a polynomial :-** The exponent in the term with the highest power is called the degree of a polynomial.
8. **Linear polynomial :-** It is a polynomial of degree 1. **Example,** $px + q, p \neq 0$.
9. **Quadratic polynomial :-** It is a polynomial of degree 2.

   Example $px^2 + qx + r, p \neq 0$

10. **Cube polynomial :-** It is a polynomial of degree 3.

    Example, $px^3 + qx^2 + rx + 5, p \neq 0$

11. **Biquadratic polynomial :-** It is a polynomial of degree 4.

    Example, $px^4 + qx^3 + rx + 3, p \neq 0$

12. **Equal polynomial :-** Two polynomial of the same degree n given by

$$p_0x^n + p_1x^{n-1} + p_2x^{n-2} + ... + p_{n-1}x + p_n$$

and $q_0x^n + q_1x^{n-1} + q_2x^{n-2} + ... + q_{n-1}x + q_n$

area said to be equal if $p_0 = q_0$, $p_1 = q_1, ..., p_n = q_n$

13. A zero of a polynomial need not be 0.
14. 0 may be a zero of a polynomial.
15. Every linear polynomial has one and only one zero.
16. A polynomial has more than one zeros.

CHAPTER 3

CO-ORDINATE GEOMETRY

French Mathematician and philosopher 'Rene' Descartes' introduced a new concept in geometry. He represented the points in a plane by ordered pairs of real number, called Cartesian co-ordinates. Cartesian coordinate is named after his name Rene Des Cartes. This branch of mathematics in which methods of algebra are used to solve geometrical problems is known as co-ordinate geometry.

Cartesian Co-ordinate System

Cartesian or Rectangular Co-ordinate Axes

In the given figure, XOX′ and YOY′ are two mutually perpendicular lines through a point O.

X-axis. The horizontal line XOX′ is called *x*-axis or axis of *x*.

Note: X-coordinate is called the abscissa

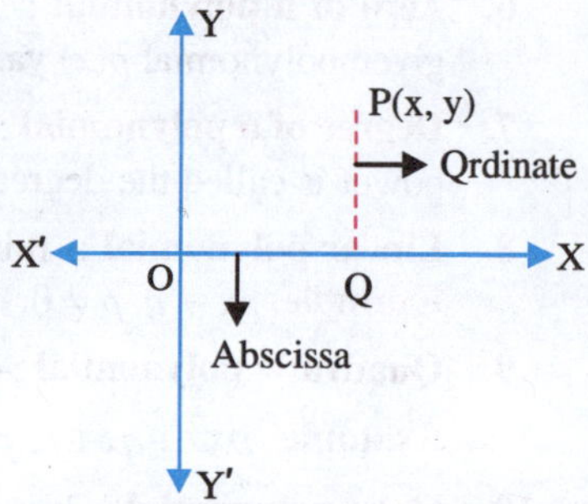

Y-axis. The vertical line YOY′ is called *y*-axis or axis of *y*.

Note: Y-coordinate is called the ordinate

Co-ordinates axes

The two lines XOX′ and YOY′ together are called co-ordinates axes or axes. The point O is called the origin.

Quadrants

The two axes XOX′ and XOY′ divide the plane into four regions, called quadrants. The quadrants are ned as follows

XOY → I Quadrant; YOX′ → II Quadrant

X′OY′ → III Quadrant; Y′OX → IV Quadrant

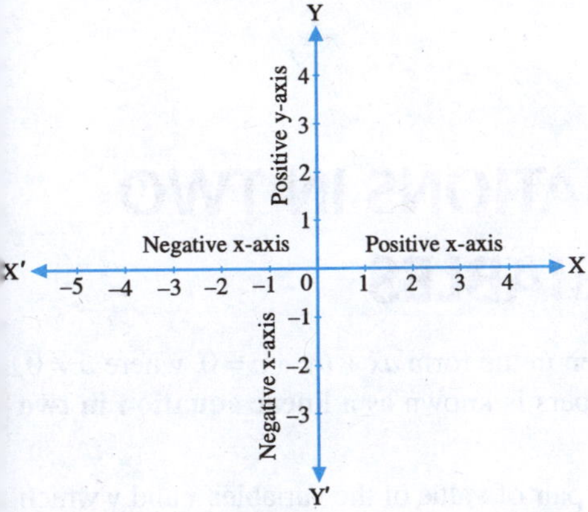

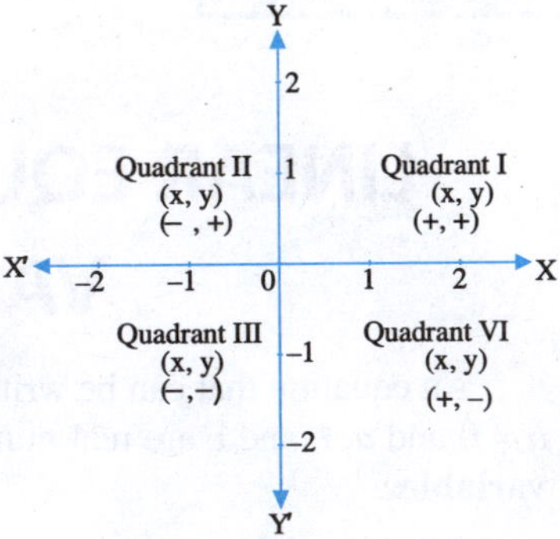

Origin

The point of intersection of two perpendicular lines is known as origin O (0,0).

Equation

(*i*) Equation of x-axis is $y = 0$

(*ii*) Equation of y- axis is $x = 0$

Graph

(*i*) The line $x = a$ is always parallel to y- axis.

(*ii*) The line $y = a$ is always parallel to x- axis.

Plotting of Point

In this section, we shall know about the plotting of points with given integral co-ordinates.

Example : (*i*) (2, 1) (*ii*) (–2, – 2)

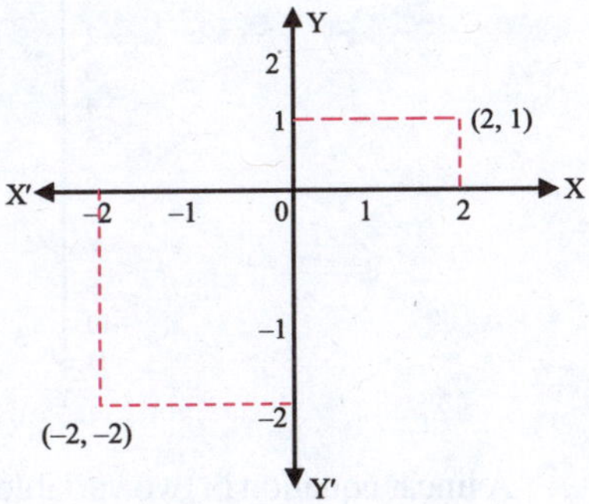

CHAPTER 4

LINEAR EQUATIONS IN TWO VARIABLES

An equation that can be written in the form $ax + by + c = 0$, where $a \neq 0$, $b \neq 0$ and a, b and c are real numbers is known as a **linear equation in two variables.**

Solution of linear equation: A pair of value of the variables x and y which satisfy the linear equation $ax + by + c = 0$ is **called a solution of the equation.**

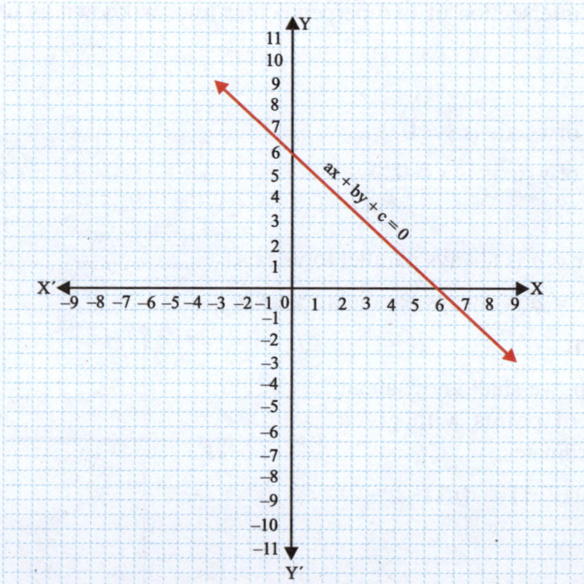

A linear equation in two variables has infinitely many solutions.

The graph of every linear equation in two variables is a straight line.

The graph of $y = 0$ represents the x-axis and $x = 0$ represents the y-axis.

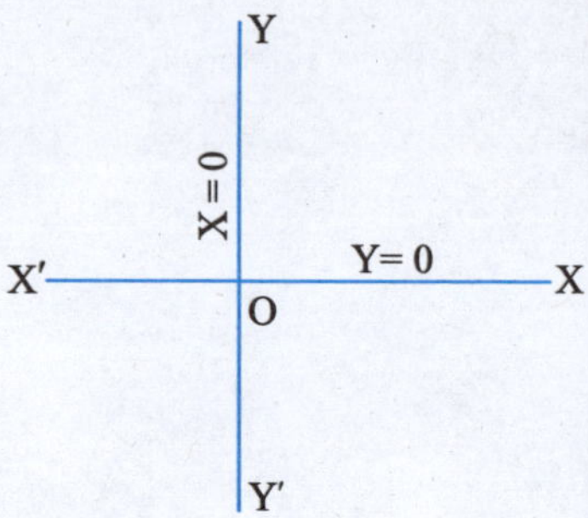

The graph of the equation $x = a$ is a straight line parallel to the y-axis and is at a distance of 'a' units from it.

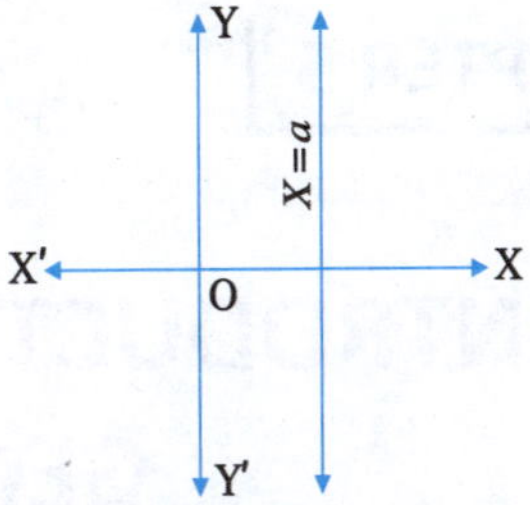

The graph of the equation $y = b$ is a straight line parallel to the x-axis and is at a distance of 'b' units from it.

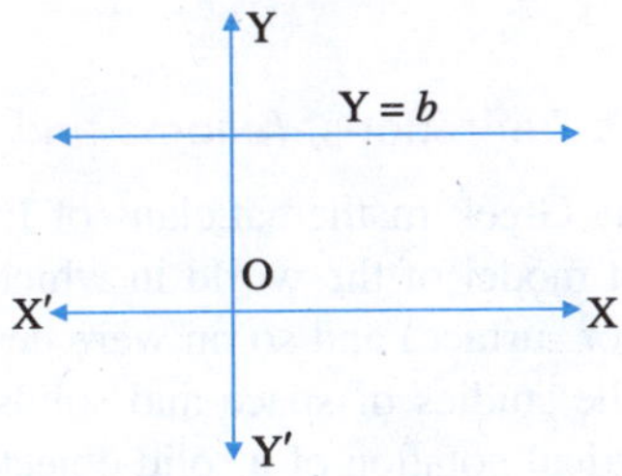

An equation is of the form $y = mx$ represents a straight line passing through the origin.

Every point on the graph of a linear equation in two variables is a solution of the linear equation. Every solution of a linear equation is a point on the graph of a linear equation.

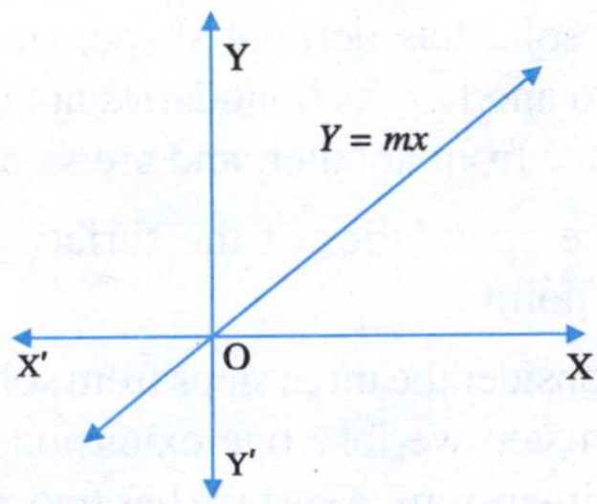

POINTS TO REMEMBER

1. An equation of the form $ax + by + c = 0$ is linear in two variables x and y for all a and b are the coefficients of x and y respectively, such that $a, b, \in \mathbf{R}$ and $a \neq 0, b \neq 0$.
2. The graph of a linear equation in two variables is a straight line.
3. A linear equation in two variables has infinitely many solutions.
4. Slope of the line $ax + by + c = 0$ is $-\dfrac{a}{b}$.
5. Equation of x-axis is $y = 0$ and equation of y-axis is $x = 0$.
6. The graph of the line $x = a$ is parallel to y-axis.
7. The graph of the line $y = b$ is parallel to x-axis.
8. Every point on the graph of a linear equation in two variables is a solution of the equation. Conversely, every solution of the linear equation in two variables represents a point on the graph of the equation.

CHAPTER 5

INTRODUCTION TO EUCLID'S GEOMETRY

Euclid's Definitions, Axioms and Postulates

The Greek mathematicians of Euclid's time thought of geometry as an abstract model of the world in which they lived. The notions of point, line, plane (or surface) and so on were derived from what was seen around them. From the studies of space and solids in the space around them, an abstract geometrical notation of a solid object was developed.

A solid has definite shape, size, position, and can be moved from one place to another. Its boundaries are called **surfaces**. They separate one part of the space from another, and are said to have no thickness.

The boundaries of the surfaces are curves or straight lines. These lines end in **points**.

Consider the three steps from solids to points (solids-surfaces-lines-points). In each step we lose one extension, also called a dimension. So, a solid has three dimensions, a surface has two, a line has one and a point has none. **Euclid summarized these statements as definitions**. He began his exposition by listing 23 definitions in Book 1 of the 'Elements'. A few of them are given below:

1. A point is that which has no part.
2. A line is breadthless length.
3. The ends of a line segment are points.
4. A straight line is a line which lies evenly with the points on itself.
5. A surface has length and breadth only.
6. The edges of a surface are lines segments.
7. A plane surface is a surface which lies evenly with the straight lines on itself.

In geometry, we take a point, a line and a plane (in Euclid's words a plane surface) as undefined terms.

Starting with his definitions, Euclid assumed certain properties, which were not to be proved. These assumptions are actually **'obvious universal truths'**. He divided them into two types: **Axioms** and **Postulates**.

He used the term **'postulate'** for the assumptions that were specific to geometry. Common notions (often called axioms), on the other hand, were assumptions used throughout mathematics and not specifically linked to geometry.

Some of Euclid's axioms, not in his order, are given below :

1. Things which are equal to the same thing are equal to one another.
2. If equals are added to equals, the wholes are equal.
3. If equals are subtracted from equals, the remainders are equal.
4. Things which coincide with one another are equal to one another.
5. The whole is greater than the part.
6. Things which are double of the same things are equal to one another.
7. Things which are halves of the same things are equal to one another.

Now let us discuss Euclid's five postulates. They are :

AXIOMS

The basic facts which are taken for granted without proof are called **Accepted facts** or **Axioms.**

Postulate 1 : A straight line may be drawn from any one point to any other point.

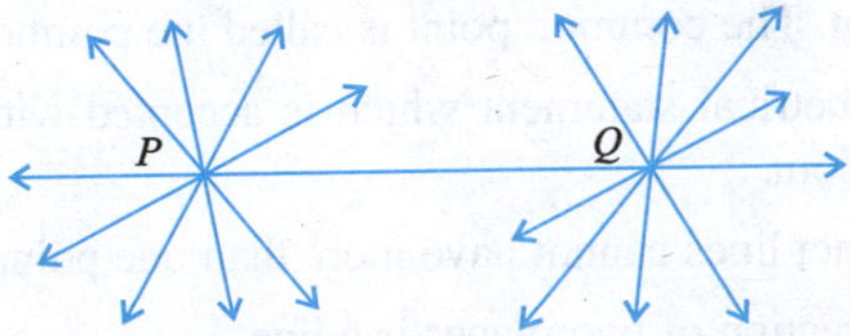

Postulate 2 : A terminated line can be produced indefinitely.

Postulate 3 : A circle can be drawn with any centre and any radius.

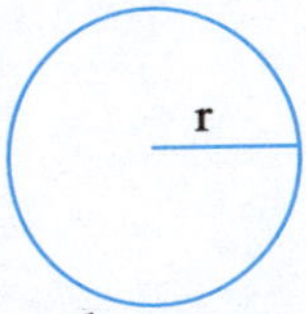

Postulate 4 : All right angles are equal to one another.

$\angle B = \angle R = 90°$

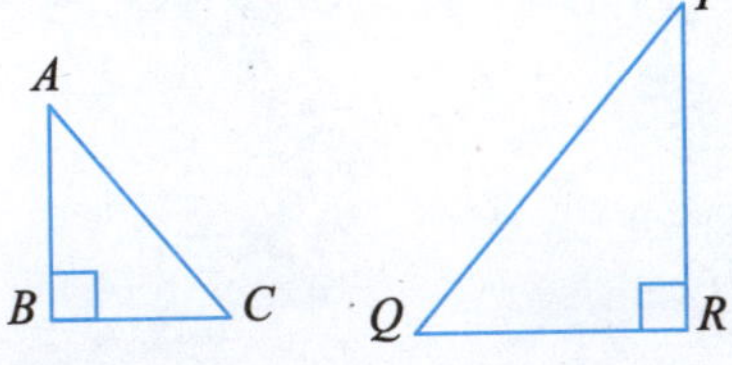

Postulate 5 : If a straight line falling on two straight lines makes the interior angles on the same side of it taken together less than two right angles, then the two straight lines, if produced indefinitely, meet on that side on which the sum of angles is less than two right angles.

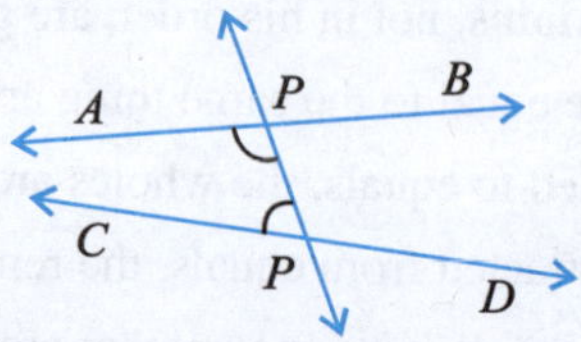

POINTS TO REMEMBER

1. A point, a line and a plane are the three basic concepts in geometry.
2. A line segment has fixed length.
3. Three or more points lying on the same straight line are called collinear.
4. Two co-planar lines are said to be parallel if they do not meet at any point on extending backward or forward.
5. Two lines are said to be intersecting when these exist a single common point.
6. Three or more lines passing through the same point are called concurrent. The common point is called the point of concurrency.
7. Any geometrical statement which is accepted without any proof is called Axiom.
8. Two distinct lines cannot have more than one point in common.
9. The intersection of two planes is a line.

CHAPTER 6

LINES AND ANGLES

The credit for introducing geometrical concepts goes to distinguished Greek mathematician Euclid (Alexandria, 300BC) known as the father of geometry.

Introduction

The word 'geometry' comes from the Greek words 'geo' meaning earth and 'metrein' meaning to measure.

Axioms

The basic facts which are taken for granted without proof, are called Accepted facts or Axioms.

Statement

A sentence which can be judged to be true or false is called a statement.

Theorems

A statement that requires a proof is called a theorem. Establishing the truth of a theorem is known as proving the theorem.

Point

A point is an exact location.

A fine dot represents a point. • P

We denote a point by a capital letter – A, B, C, D, etc.

Line Segment

A **line segment** is a part of a **line** with two end points.

Line

A **line** is a collection of points along a straight path. A **line** has no end points.

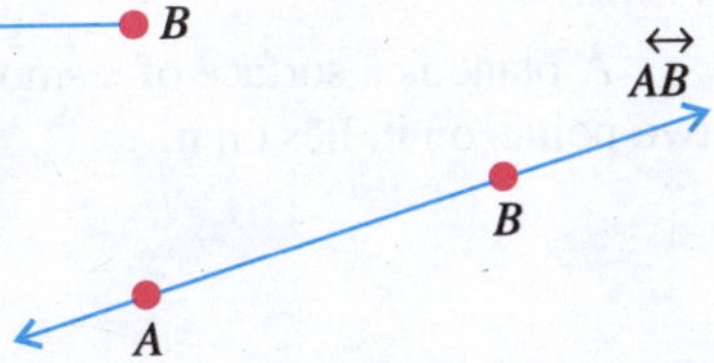

Ray

A part **of line** with one end point is called a **ray**.

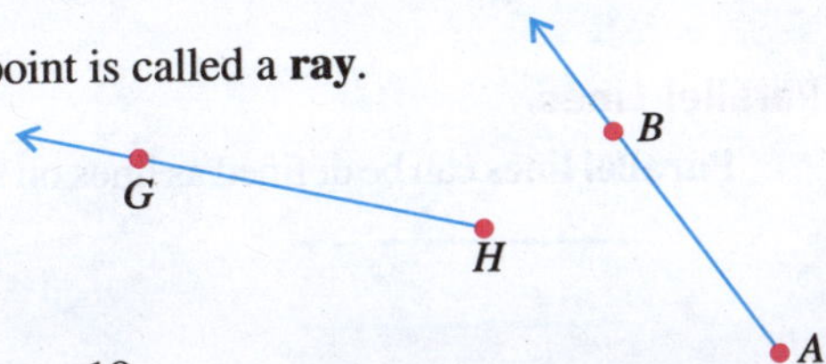

Two rays $\overrightarrow{AB}$ and $\overrightarrow{CA}$ are said to be opposite rays if A, B, C are collinear and A is the only common point of the rays.

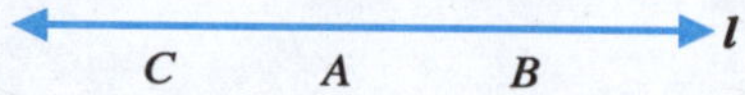

Collinear Points

All the points that lie on the same **line** are **collinear points**.

In the given point P, Q, R noncollinear

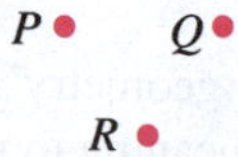

Note: Two points are trivially collinear since two points determine a line

Intersecting Lines

Intersecting lines can be defined as two or more lines that meet at one point.

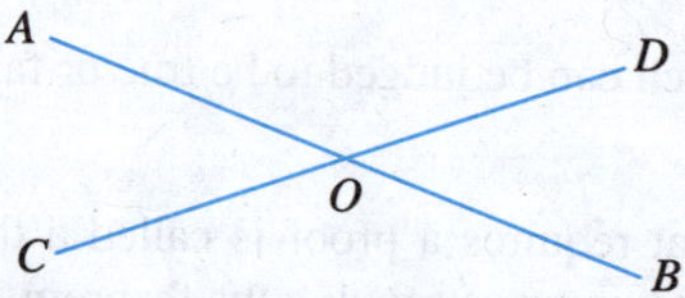

Concurrent Lines

Three or more lines intersecting at the same point are said to be concurrent.

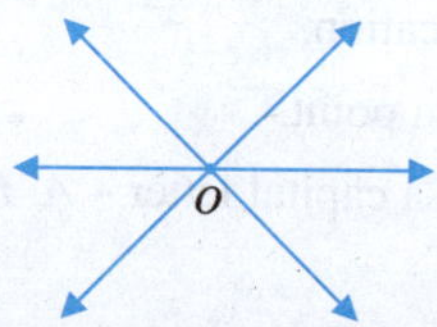

Here, O is called the point of concurrence.

Plane

A plane is a surface of a smooth wall; the surface of the line joining any two points on it, lies on it.

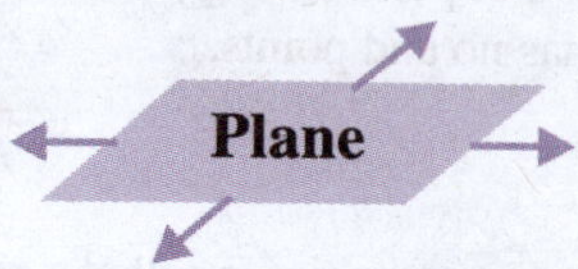

Parallel Lines

Parallel lines can be defined as lines on the same plane that never intersect.

ANGLES AND THEIR PROPERTIES

Angles

Consider the two **rays** AB and AC originating from the same point A. The union of two **rays** AB and AC is called an **angle.**

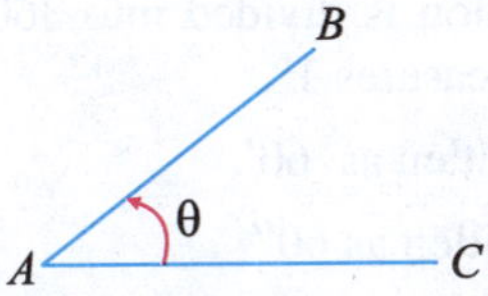

Lines AB and AC meet at the point A to form an angle. The point A is the vertex of the angle, and the lines AB and AC that make the angle are called the **arms of the angle**.

Interior and Exterior of an Angle

The interior of $\angle AOB$ is the set of all points in its plane, which lie on the same side of OA as B and also on the same side of OB as A, *e.g.* P is a point in the interior of $\angle AOB$. Any point on any arm or vertex is said to lie on angles *e.g.*, Q is a point on $\angle AOB$.

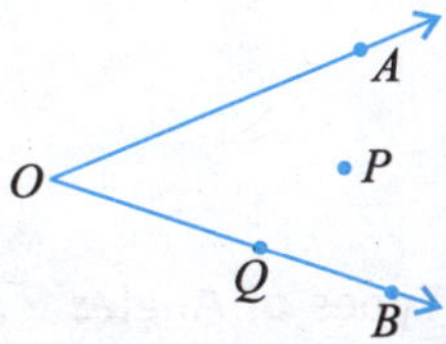

Exterior of an Angle

The exterior of an angle $\angle AOB$ is the set of all those points in its plane, which do not lie on the angle or its interior. In the following figure, R is a point in the exterior of $\angle AOB$.

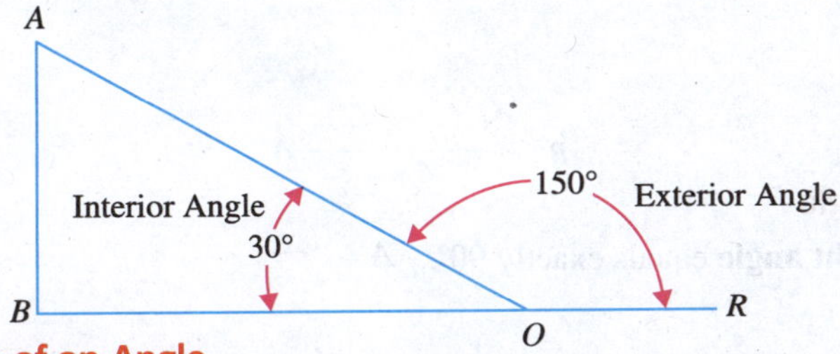

Measure of an Angle

The amount of turning from OA to OB is called the measure of $\angle AOB$, written as $m \angle AOB$.

An angle is measured in degrees and denoted by (degree).

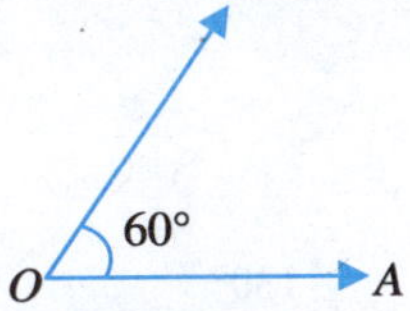

For example, $m\ (< AOB) = 60°$

An Angle of 360° (Complete Angle)

The size of an angle is measured in **degrees**; and the symbol used to represent degree is °. There are 360° in a full turn (or circle).

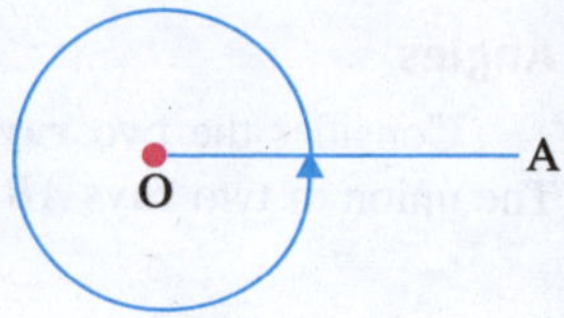

This complete rotation is divided into 360° equal parts. Each part measures 1°.

1° = 60 minutes, written as 60′.

1′ = 60 seconds, written as 60″

We use a protractor to measure an angle.

Size of an Angle

The amount of turn from one arm of the angle to the other is said to be the **size of an angle.**

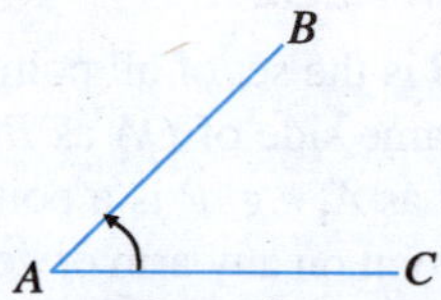

Types of Angles

Angles are classified according to their size as follows:

Acute Angle

An **acute angle** is greater than 0° and less than 90°.

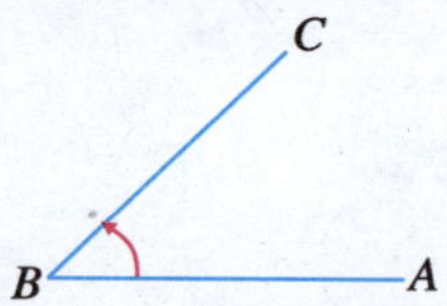

Right Angle

A **right angle** equals exactly 90°.

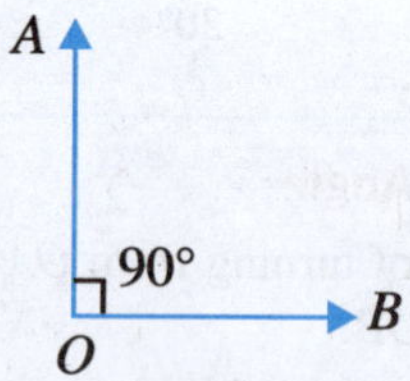

Obtuse Angle

Angles **greater than 90 degrees** but **less than 180 degrees** are known as **obtuse angles.**

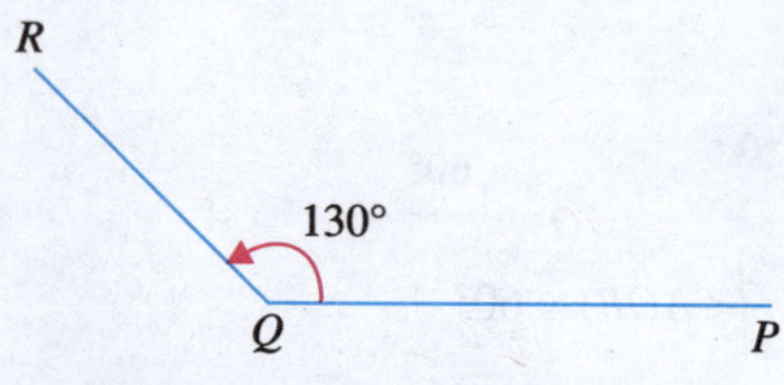

Straight Angle

An angle which is **equal to 180 degrees** is called a **straight angle.**

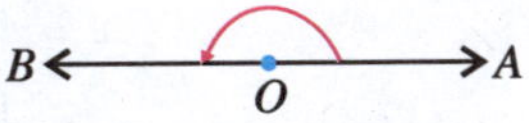

Reflex Angle

A **reflex angle** is **greater than 180 degrees** but **less than 360 degrees.**

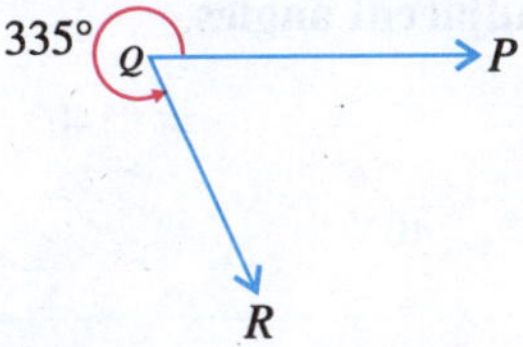

Adjacent Angle

Two **angles** are said to be adjacent if they have a common arm and a common vertex, and their non-common arms are on the different sides of the common arm. In fig below,

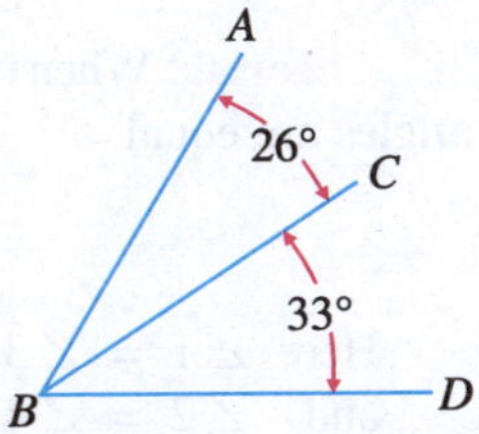

$\angle ABC$ is adjacent to $\angle CBD$

Because:

- they have a common arm (line *CB*).
- they have a common vertex (point *B*).

Linear Pair of Angles

Linear pair of angles: Two **adjacent angles** are said to form a **linear pair** if their **sum is 180°**

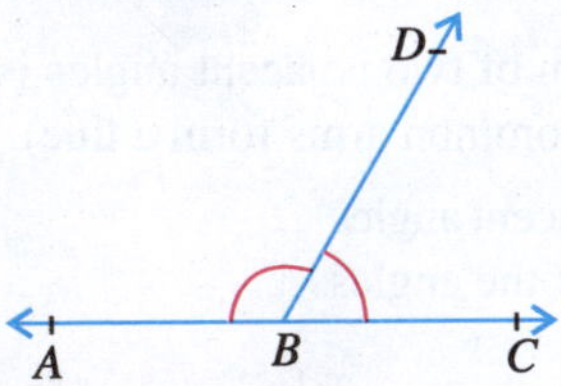

Vertically Opposite Angles

Vertically opposite angles: When two lines intersect, four angles are formed. The angles that are opposite to each other are called **vertically opposite angles.**

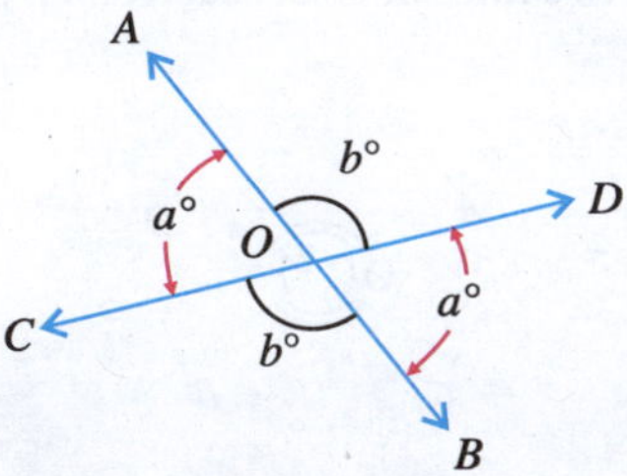

Complementary Angles

Two angles are said to be **complementary,** if their sum is 90°.

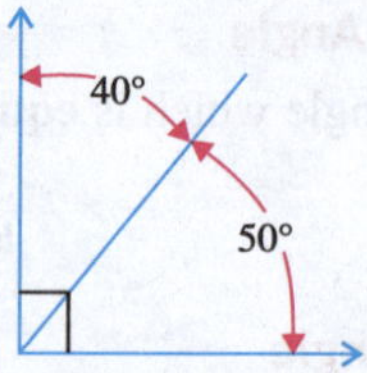

Supplementary Angles

Two angles are **supplementary** if their sum is 180 degrees. They may or may not be **adjacent angles.**

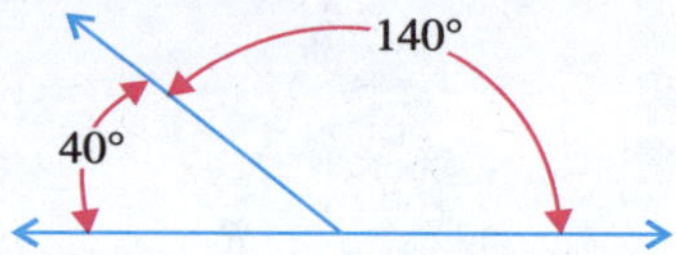

Theorem: When two **lines** intersect each other, then the **vertically opposite angles** are equal.

Here, ∠1 = ∠3
and ∠2 = ∠4

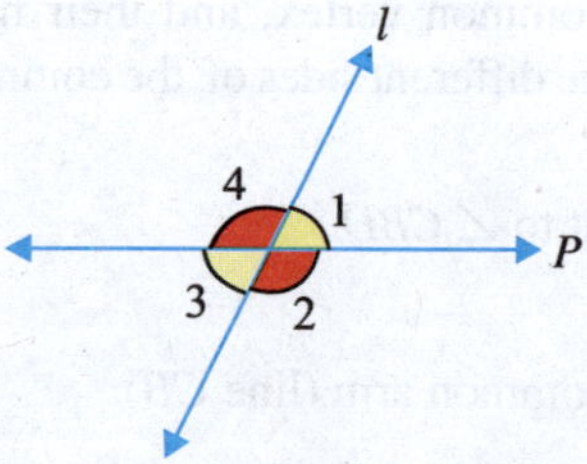

Pairs of Angles

Axiom 6.1 : If a ray stands on a line, then the sum of two adjacent angles so formed is 180°. When the sum of two adjacent angles is 180°, then they are called **a linear pair of angles.**

We may also write that if the sum of two adjacent angles is 180°, then a ray stands on a line (that is, the non-common arms form a line).

Axiom 6.2 : If the sum of two adjacent angles is 180°, then the non-common arms of the angles form a line.

If $\angle x + \angle y = 180° \Rightarrow AOB$ is a straight line.

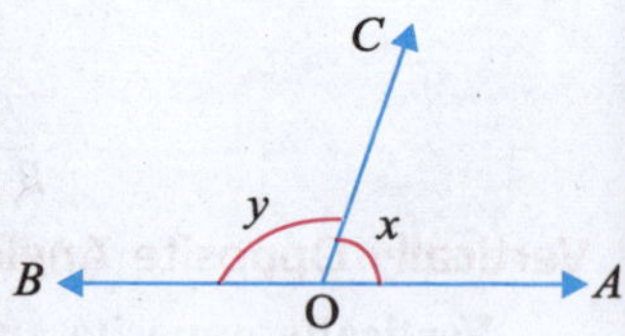

The two axioms above together is called the Linear Pair Axiom

Theorem 6.1 : If two lines intersect each other, then the vertically opposite angles are equal.

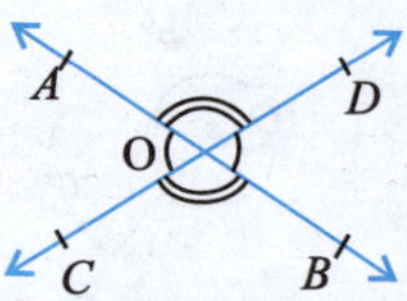

Parallel Lines and a Transversal

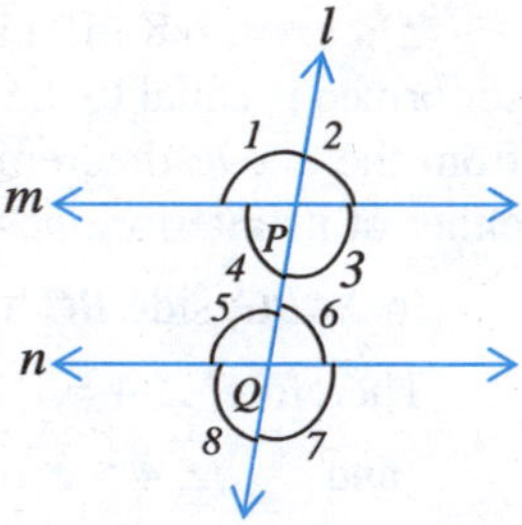

A line which intersects two or more lines at distinct points is called a **transversal** (see Fig.). Line l intersects lines m and n at points P and Q respectively. Therefore, line l is a transversal for lines m and n.

(*a*) **Corresponding angles**

(*i*) $\angle 1$ and $\angle 5$ (*ii*) $\angle 2$ and $\angle 6$

(*iii*) $\angle 4$ and $\angle 8$ (*iv*) $\angle 3$ and $\angle 7$

(*b*) **Alternate interior angles** :

(*i*) $\angle 4$ and $\angle 6$ (*ii*) $\angle 3$ and $\angle 5$

(*c*) **Alternate exterior angles**:

(*i*) $\angle 1$ and $\angle 7$ (*ii*) $\angle 2$ and $\angle 8$

(*d*) **Interior angles on the same side of the transversal**:

(*i*) $\angle 4$ and $\angle 5$ (*ii*) $\angle 3$ and $\angle 6$

Interior angles on the same side of the transversal are also referred to as consecutive interior angles or allied angles or co-interior angles.

Axiom 6.3 : If a transversal intersects two parallel lines, then each pair of corresponding angles are equal. Axiom 6.3 is also referred to as the corresponding angles axiom.

Axiom 6.4 : If a transversal intersects two lines such that a pair of corresponding angles are equal, then the two lines are parallel to each other.

Theorem 6.2 : If a transversal intersects two parallel lines, then each pair of alternate interior angles are equal.

Theorem 6.3 : If a transversal intersects two lines such that a pair of alternate interior angles are equal, then the two lines are parallel.

Theorem 6.4 : If a transversal intersects two parallel lines, then each pair of interior angles on the same side of the transversal is supplementary.

Theorem 6.5 : If a transversal intersects two lines such that a pair of interior angles on the same side of the transversal is supplementary, then the two lines are parallel.

Lines Parallel to the Same Line

Theorem 6.6 : Lines which are parallel to the same line are parallel to each other.

Angle Sum Property of a Triangle

Theorem 6.7 : The sum of the three angles of a triangle is 180º.

$$\angle A + \angle B + \angle C = 180°$$

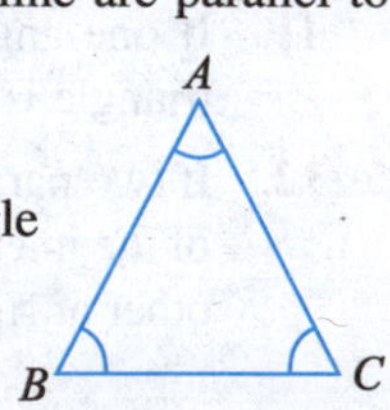

Theorem 6.8 : If a side of a triangle is produced, then the exterior angle so formed is equal to the sum of the two interior opposite angles. It is obvious from the above theorem that an exterior angle of a triangle is greater than either of its interior opposite angles.

In ΔABC, side BC has been produced to D forming exterior angle $\angle 4$

Therefore, $\angle 4 = \angle 1 + \angle 3$

and $\quad \angle 4 > \angle 1, \ \angle 4 > \angle 3$

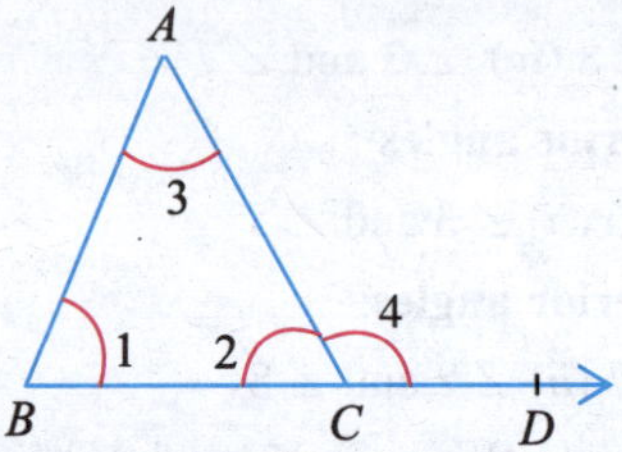

POINTS TO REMEMBER

1. Two intersecting lines cannot both be equal and parallel to the same line.
2. If a ray stands on a line, then the sum of two adjacent angles so formed is 180°.
3. If the sum of two adjacent angles is 180°, then the non-common arms of two angles are two opposite rays.
4. If two lines intersect, the vertically opposite angles are equal.
5. Lines which are parallel to the same line are parallel to each other.
6. The bisectors of two adjacent supplementary angles form a right angle.
7. If two parallel lines are cut by a transversal, the pairs of alternate angles are equal.
8. If two parallel lines are cut by a transversal, the pairs of corresponding angles are equal.
9. The sum of three angles of a triangle is 180°.
10. If a side of a triangle is produced, the exterior angle so formed is equal to the sum of two interior opposite angles.
11. If one angle of a triangle is equal to the sum of the other two, the triangle is right angled.
12. If two parallel lines are intersected by a transversal then the bisectors of the interior angles on the same side of the transversal intersect each other at right angles.

CHAPTER 7

TRIANGLES

1. Two figures are congruent, if they are of the same shape and of the same size.

2. Two circles of the same radii are congruent.

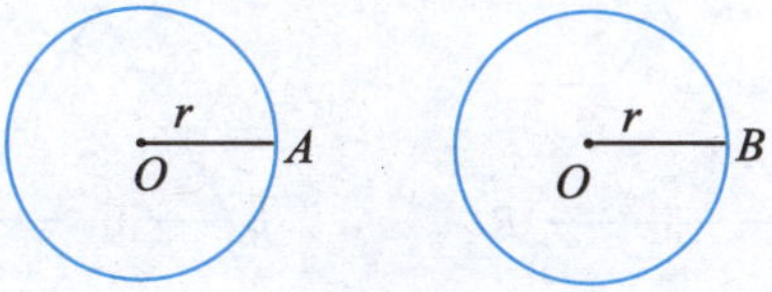

3. Two squares of the same sides are congruent.

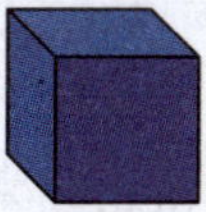

4. If two triangles ABC and PQR are congruent under the correspondence $AB \leftrightarrow PQ$, $BC \leftrightarrow QR$ and $CA \leftrightarrow RP$, then symbolically, it is expressed as $\Delta ABC \cong \Delta PQR$.

5. **SAS Congruence Rule:** Two triangles are congruent if two sides and the included angle of one triangle are equal to the two sides and the included angle of the other triangle.

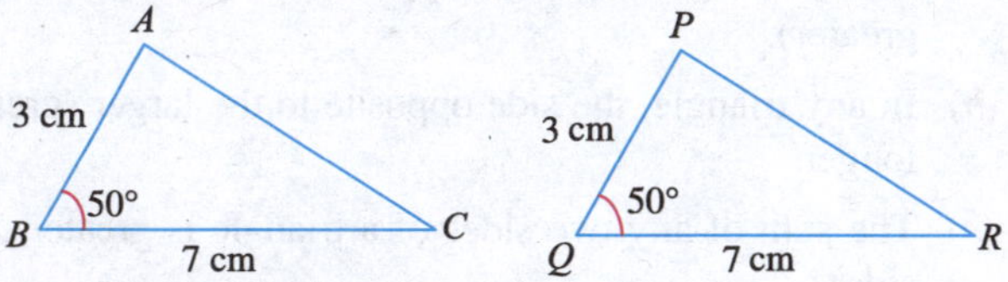

6. **ASA Congruence Rule:** Two triangles are congruent if two angles and the included side of one triangle are equal to two angles and the included side of other triangle.

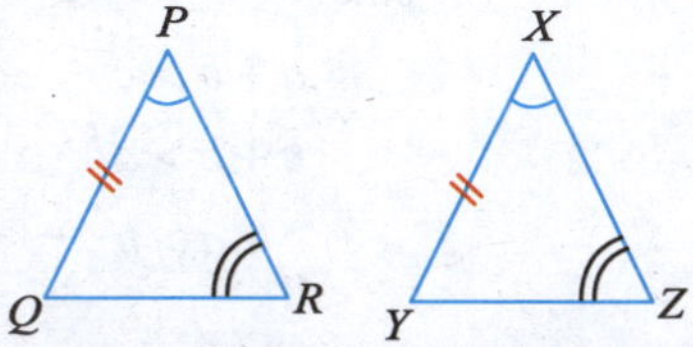

7. **AAS Congruence Rule:** Two triangles are congruent if any two pairs of angles and one pair of corresponding sides are equal.

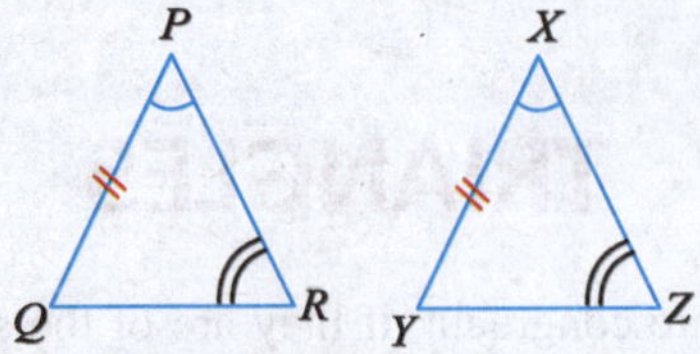

8. **Some Properties of a Triangle:**
   (*a*) Angles opposite to equal sides of a triangle are equal.
   (*b*) The sides opposite to equal angles of a triangle are equal.

9. **SSS Congruence Rule:** If three sides of one triangle are equal to the three sides of another triangle, then the two triangles are congruent.

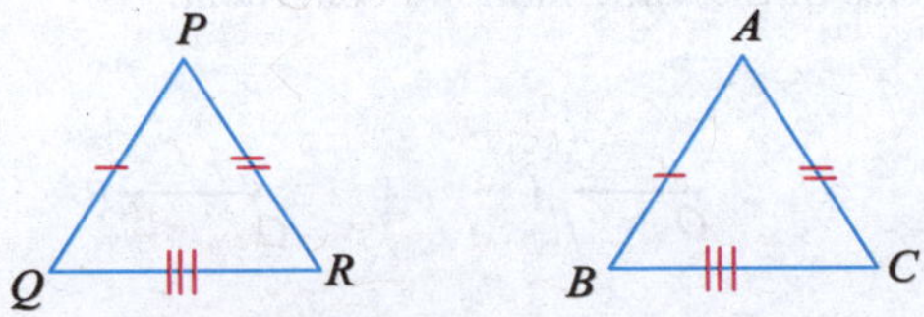

10. **RHS Congruence Rule:** If in two right triangles the hypotenuse and one side of one triangle are equal to the hypotenuse and one side of the other triangle, then the two triangles are congruent.

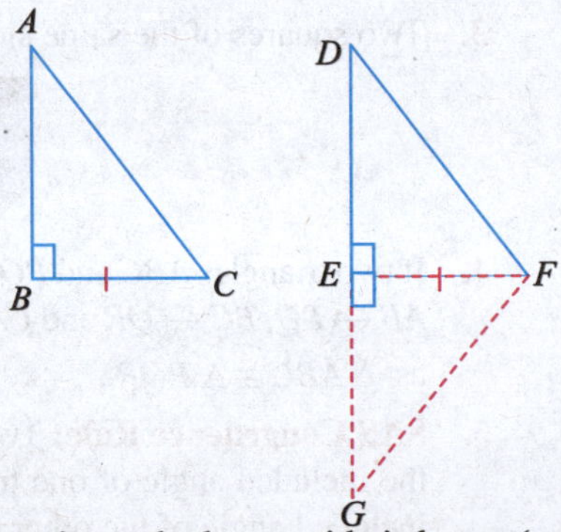

RHS stands for Right angle - Hypotenuse - Side.

11. **Inequalities in a Triangle**
   (*a*) In any triangle, the angle opposite to the longer side is larger (or greater).
   (*b*) In any triangle, the side opposite to the larger (greater) angle is longer.
   (*c*) The sum of any two sides of a triangle is greater than the third side.

$a + b > c$

$b + c > a$

$c + a > b$

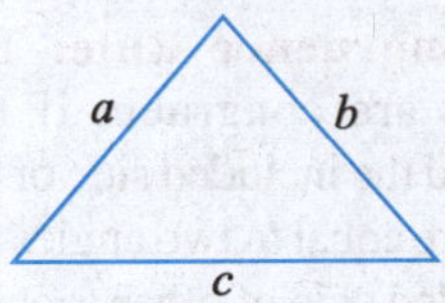

POINTS TO REMEMBER

1. Two triangles are congruent if the three sides of one triangle are equal to the three sides of the other triangle.
2. The angles opposite to equal sides of a triangle are equal.
3. The sides opposite to equal angles of a triangle are equal.
4. If the bisector of vertical angle of a triangle is perpendicular to the base of triangle then the triangle is isosceles.
5. A triangle ABC is isosceles if and only if any two altitudes are equal.
6. If two sides of a triangle are unequal, the larger side has the greater angle opposite to it.
7. In a triangle, the greater angle has a larger side opposite to it.
8. The sum of any two sides of a triangle is greater than the third side.
9. Difference of any two sides of triangle is less than the third side.
10. Of all line-segments that can be drawn to a given line from a point not lying on it, the perpendicular line-segment is the shortest.
11. If the altitude from the vertex of a triangle bisects the opposite side, then the triangle is isosceles.
12. The medians of an equilateral triangle are equal.
13. The sum of three altitudes of a triangle is less than the sum of the three sides of the triangle.
14. The sum of any two sides of a triangle is greater than twice the median drawn to the third side.
15. The perimeter of a triangle is greater than the sum of its three medians.
16. In a right –angle triangle, the hypotenuse is the longest side.
17. A triangle can be constructed only when the sum of any two sides is greater than the third side.

CHAPTER 8

QUADRILATERALS

Quadrilateral just means "four sides" (*quad* means four, *lateral* means side).

Quadrilateral:

A quadrilateral is a plane closed figure bounded by four line-segments *AB*, *BC*, *CD* and *DA*.

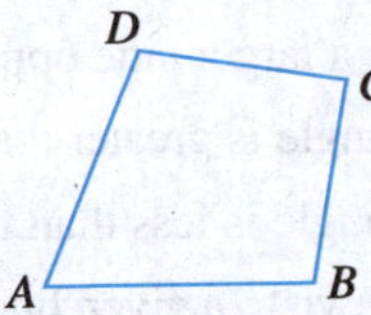

(*i*)

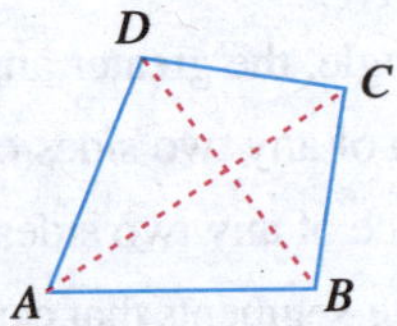

(*ii*)

Types of Quadrilaterals:

Trapezium:

A quadrilateral in which two opposite sides are parallel, namely, *AB* and *CD* and other two opposite sides are non- parallel, namely *AD* and *BC*. is called a trapezium.

If the two non-parallel sides of a trapezium are equal then it is called an isosceles trapezium.

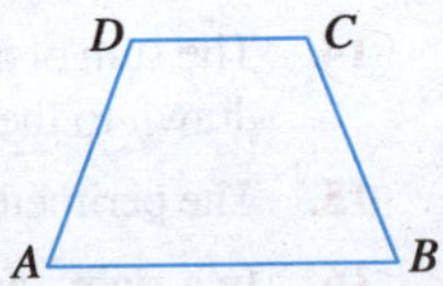

Parallelograms:

A quadrilateral in which opposite sides are parallel and equal is called a parallelogram, written as ||gm.

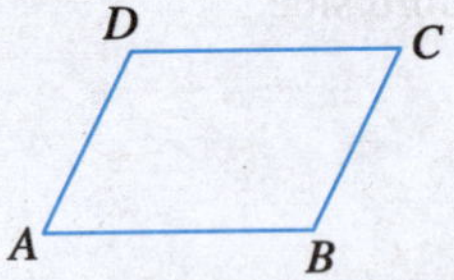

Rectangle:

A parallelogram each of whose angle is 90°, is called a rectangle, written as rect.*ABCD* etc.

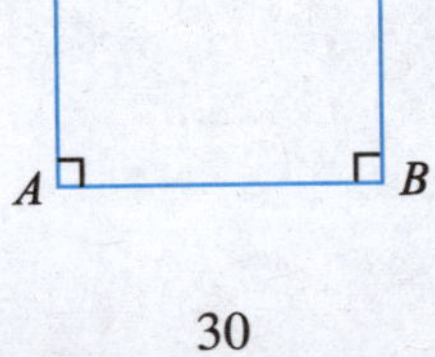

Square:

A rectangle having all sides are equal is called a square. Each angle of square is 90°.

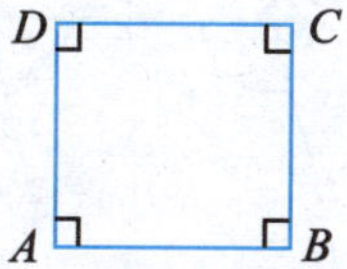

Rhombus:

A parallelogram having all sides are equal is called a rhombus.

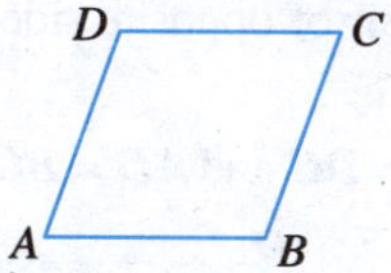

Kite:

A quadrilateral in which two pairs of adjacent sides are equal is known as kite.

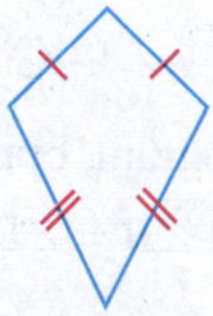

Note:

- A square, rectangle and rhombus are all parallelograms.
- A square is a rectangle and also a rhombus.
- A parallelogram is a trapezium.
- A kite is not a parallelogram.
- A trapezium is not a parallelogram (as only one pair of opposite sides are parallel in a trapezium and we require both pairs to be parallel in a parallelogram).
- A rectangle or a rhombus is not a square.

Properties of a Parallelogram

Theorem 8.1: A diagonal of a parallelogram divides it into two congruent triangles.

$$\Delta ABC \cong \Delta CDA$$

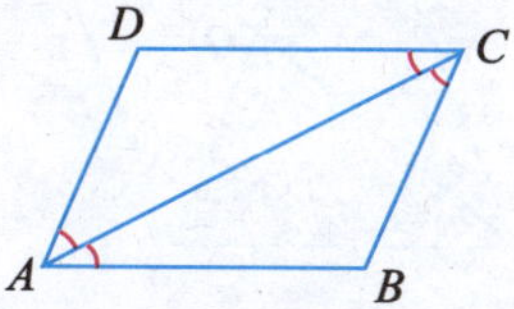

Theorem 8.2 : In a parallelogram, opposite sides are equal.

$$AB = DC \text{ and } AD = BC$$

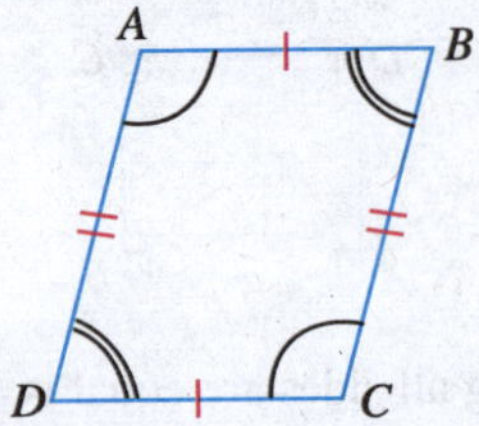

Theorem 8.3 : If both pair of opposite sides of a quadrilateral are equal, then it is a parallelogram.

$$AB = DC \text{ and } AD = BC$$

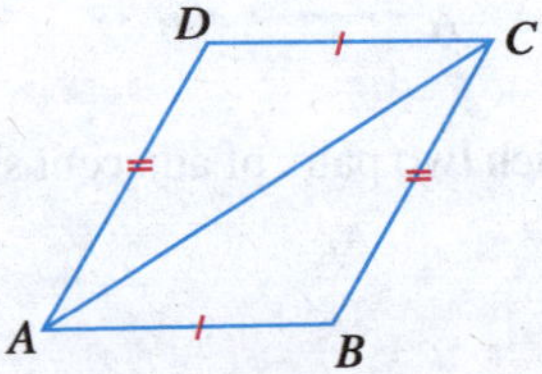

Theorem 8.4 : In a parallelogram, opposite angles are equal.

$$\angle A = \angle C \quad \text{and } \angle B = \angle D$$

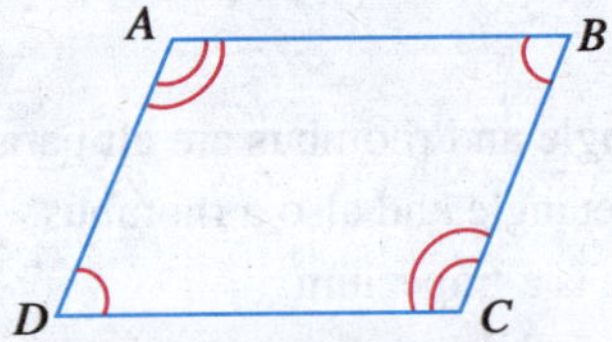

Theorem 8.5: If in a quadrilateral, both pair of opposite angles are equal, then it is a parallelogram. Quadrilateral $ABCD$ in which $\angle A = \angle C$ and $\angle B = \angle D$, is a parallelogram

Theorem 6 : The diagonals of a parallelogram bisect each other.

$$AO = OC \text{ and } DO = BO$$

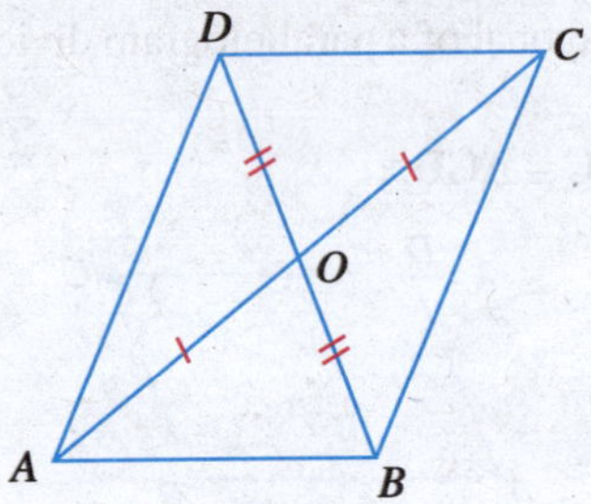

Theorem 8.7 : If the diagonals of a quadrilateral bisect each other, then it is a parallelogram. In a quadrilateral if $AO = OC$ and $DO = BO$, it is a parallelogram.

Theorem 8.8 : A quadrilateral is a parallelogram if a pair of opposite sides is equal and parallel.

$AB = DC$ and $AB \parallel DC$
$AD = BC$ and $AD \parallel BC$

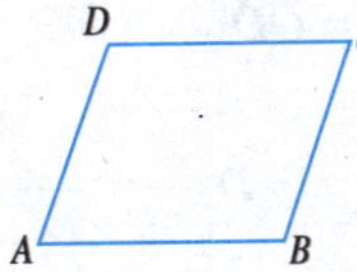

The Mid-point Theorem

Theorem 8.9 : The line segment joining the mid-points of two sides of a triangle is parallel to the third side and half of it.

In ΔABC, D is the midpoint of side AC i.e., $AD = DC$ and E is the midpoint of AB, i.e., $AE = EB$, in this case $DE \parallel BC$ and

$$DE = \frac{1}{2}BC$$

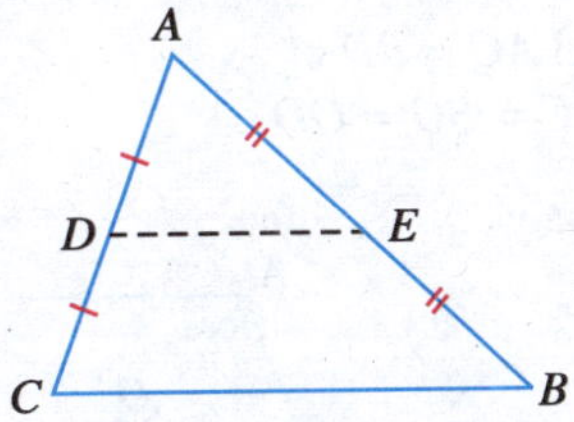

Theorem 8.10 : The line drawn through the mid-point of one side of a triangle, parallel to another side bisects the third side.

In ΔABC, if D is the midpoint of side AC, $AD = DC$ and $DE \parallel BC$ then E will be the midpoint of AB, i.e., $AE = EB$, in this case

$$DE = \frac{1}{2}BC$$

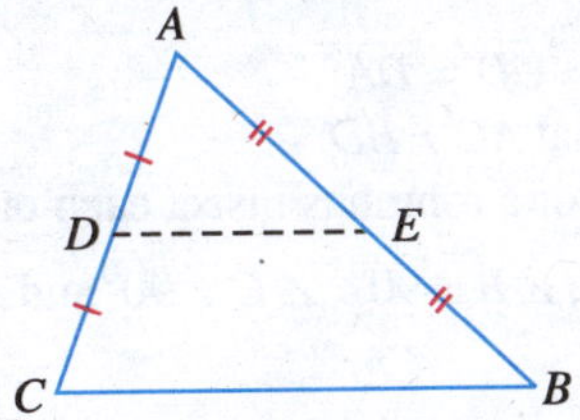

Rectangle

The diagonals of a rectangle are of equal length.

$AC = BD$

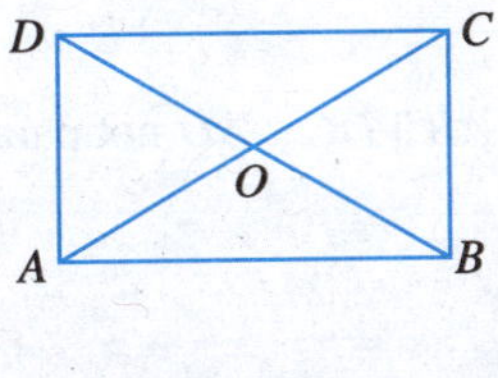

Note : Properties of rectangle

* $\angle A = \angle B = \angle C = \angle D = 90^0$
* $AB = CD$ and $AD = BC$
* Diagonal $AC = BD$
* $AO = OC = BO = OD$

Square

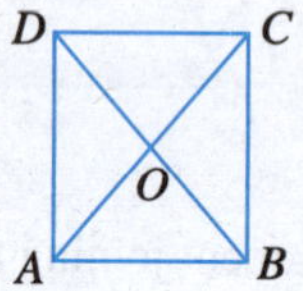

Properties of a Square : All the sides of a square are equal i.e.,

$AB = BC = CD = DA$

* $\angle A = 90^0, \angle B = 90^0, \angle C = 90^0$ and $\angle D = 90^0$
* diagonal $AC = BD$
* $AO = OC = BO = OD$

Rhombus

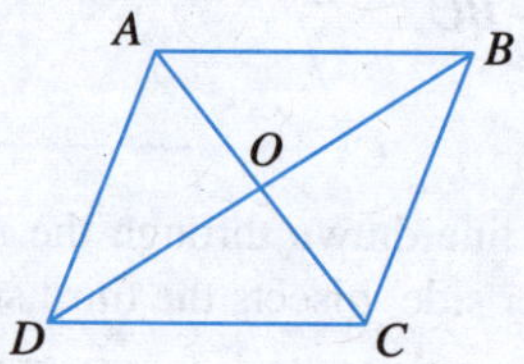

Properties of Rhombus:- All the sides of a rhombus are equal in length *i.e.*,

* $AB = BC = CD = DA$
* But diagonal $AC \neq BD$
* Diagonals of a rohmbus bisect each other at 90°
* $\angle A \neq 90^0, \angle B \neq 90^0, \angle C \neq 90^0$ and $\angle D \neq 90^0$

Trapezium

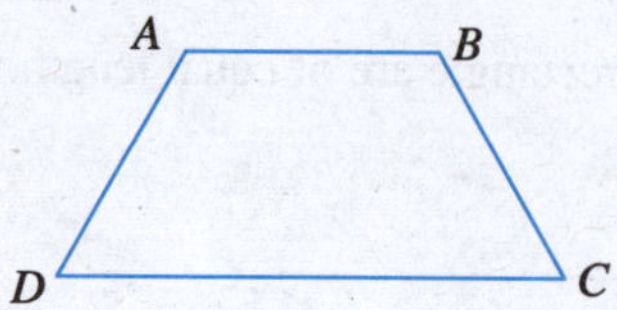

Properties of Trapezium: - $AB \parallel DC$, ***AD*** not parallel ***BC*.**

POINTS TO REMEMBER

1. A quadrilateral is a plane closed figure bounded by four line-segments.
2. The sum of all angles of a quadrilateral is 360°.
3. A diagonal of a parallelogram divides it into two congruent triangles.
4. In a parallelogram, the opposite sides are of equal length and its converse.
5. In a parallelogram, the opposite angles are equal and its converse.
6. A quadrilateral is a parallelogram, if a pair of its opposite sides is parallel and is of equal length.
7. In a parallelogram, the diagonals bisect each other and its converse.
8. A parallelogram is a rectangle, if its diagonals have equal length and its converse.
9. A parallelogram is a rhombus, if its diagonals are perpendicular and its converse.
10. A parallelogram is a square, if its diagonal are equal and are at right angles and its converse.
11. In a triangle, the line segment joining the mid points of any two sides is parallel to the third side and is half of it.
12. The line drawn through the mid point of one side of a triangle parallel to another side bisects the third side.
13. If there are three or more parallel lines and the intercepts made by them on a transversal are equal, the corresponding intercepts made on other transversal are also equal.
14. The quadrilateral formed by joining the mid points of the sides of a quadrilateral in order, is a parallelogram.
15. In a parallelogram, the bisectors of any two consecutive angles intersect at right angle.
16. A quadrilateral in which a pair of opposite sides is parallel is called a trapezium.
17. When two non-parallel sides of a trapezium are equal, we call it an isosceles trapezium.

AREAS OF PARALLELOGRAMS AND TRIANGLES

"The magnitude or measure of the planar region is called its area"

Area of plane figure is the surface enclosed by its boundary or sides. The shaded portion in the figures represent their area.

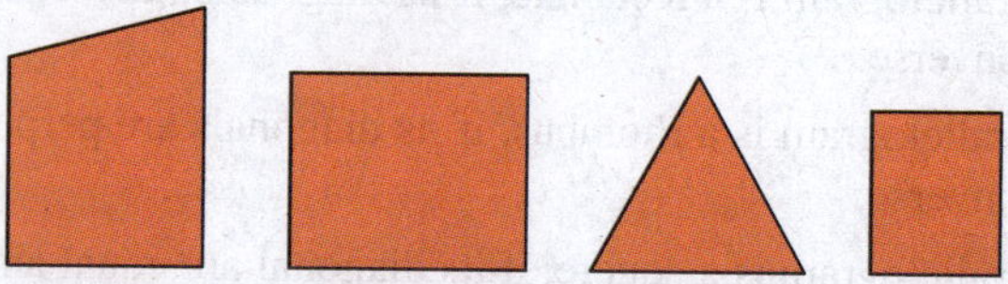

Note that Δ ABC and Δ DBE of Fig.

(*i*) are not on the common base. Similarly, Δ ABC and parallelogram PQRS of Fig.

(*ii*) are also not on the same base.

Parallelograms on the same base and between the same Parallels

Theorem 9.1: Parallelograms on the same base and between the same parallels are equal in area.

$$\text{ar}\ (||^{gm}\ ADCB) = \text{ar}\ (||^{gm}\ CDEF)$$

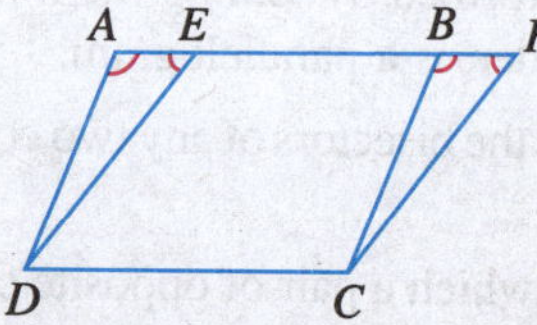

Note: area of $||^{gm}$ (parallelogram) = Base × Altitude.

* Parallelograms on the same base (or equal bases) and having equal areas lie between the same parallels.

Triangles on the same Base and between the same Parallels

Theorem 9.2 : Two triangles on the same base (or equal bases) and between the same parallels are equal in area.

area (Δ ABC) = area (Δ DBC)

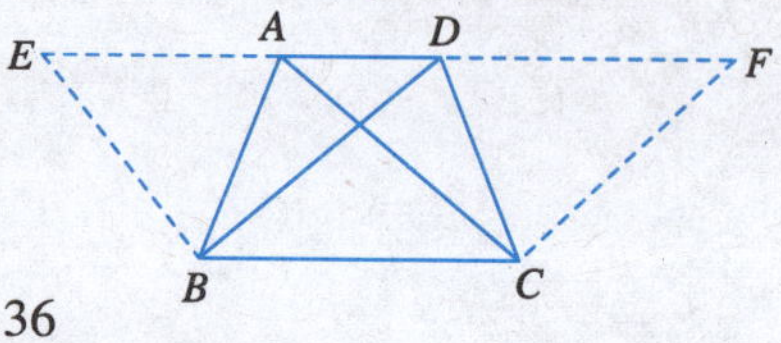

Note : Important Results

1. Area of a triangle = $\frac{1}{2} \times \text{base} \times \text{height (altitude)}$
2. Area of a trapezium
   $= \frac{1}{2} \times (\text{sum of the parallel sides}) \times (\text{Distance between them})$
3. Area of Rhombus = $\frac{1}{2} \times (\text{product of the diagonals})$

Theorem 9.3: Two triangles having the same base (or equal bases) and equal areas lie between the same parallels.

If area of Δ ABC = area of Δ DBC, then $AD \parallel BC$.

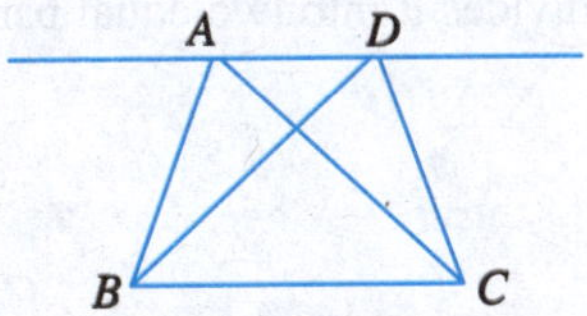

Result : A median of a triangle divides it into two triangles of equal area.

Area of ΔABD = area of ΔADC where

AD is the median of ΔABC.

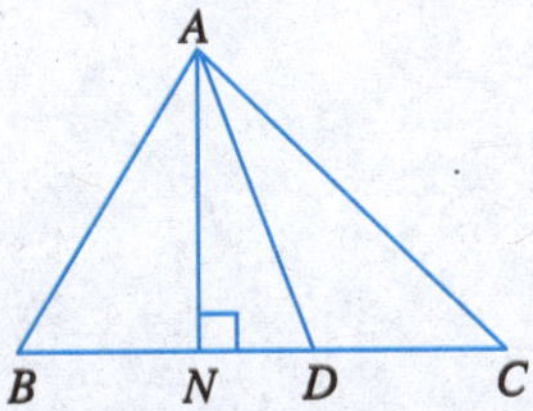

POINTS TO REMEMBER

1. Two congruent figures have equal area but the converse is not always true.
2. A diagonal of a $\|^{gm}$ divides it into two triangles of equal area.
3. Parallelograms on the same base and between the same parallels are equal in area.
4. A parallelogram and a rectangle on the same base and between the same parallels are equal in area.
5. Triangles on the same base and between the same parallels are equal in area.
6. If a triangle and a parallelogram are on the same base, and between

the same parallels, then the area of the triangle is equal to half the area of the parallelogram.

7. If two triangle have equal areas and one side of the one triangle is equal to one side of the other then their corresponding altitudes are equal.
8. A median of a triangle divides it into two triangles of equal area.
9. The diagonals of parallelogram divides it into four triangles of equal area.
10. If each diagonal of a quadrilateral separates it into two triangle of equal area then the quadrilateral is parallelogram.
11. The line segment joining the mid-points of a pair of opposite sides of a parallelogram divides it into two equal parallelograms.

CHAPTER 10

CIRCLES

Important theorems and properties:

Circle

A circle is the locus of a point which moves in a plane in such a way that its distance from a given fixed point is always constant.

The fixed point is called the centre and the constant distance is called the radius of the circle. A circle with centre O and radius r is denoted by $C(O, r)$.

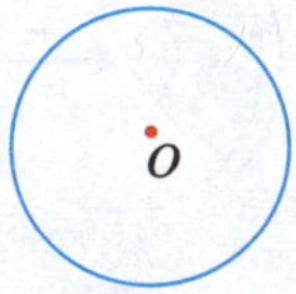

Diameter

The distance across a circle through the center is called the diameter.

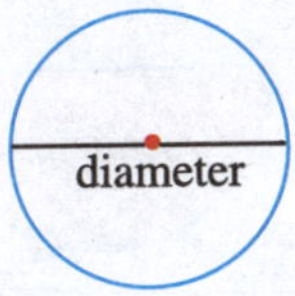

Radius

Any straight line joining the centre to a point on the circumference is called a radius. All the radii of a circle are equal.

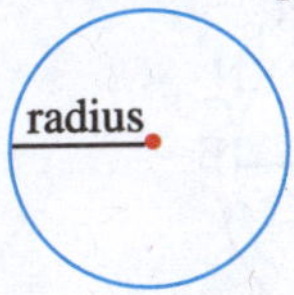

Interior and Exterior

Interior: A point lying inside a circle is called an interior point of the circle.

Exterior: A point lying outside a circle is called an exterior point of the circle.

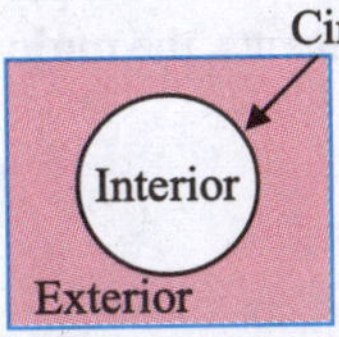

Chord of a circle

The line segment joining two points on the circle is called chord of the circle. points A and B on a circle, then the line segment AB is called the **chord** of the circle.

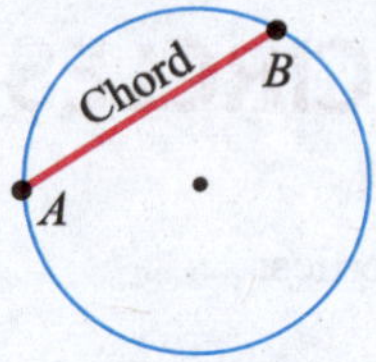

Arc of a circle

A part of a circumference between two points is called an arc. The longer part is called the major arc AB and the shorter part is called the minor arc AB.

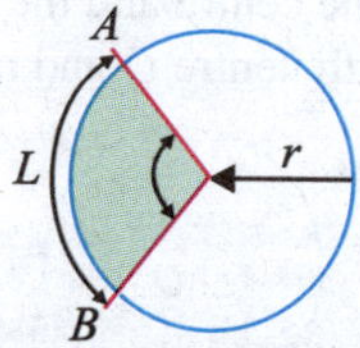

Semicircle

When P and Q are ends of a diameter, then both arcs are equal and each is called a semicircle. A diameter divides a circle in two equal parts. Each part is called a semicircle.

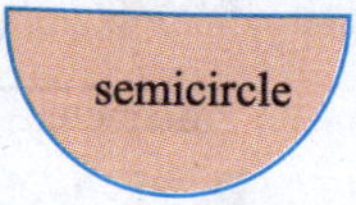

Circumference

The length of the complete circle is called its circumference.

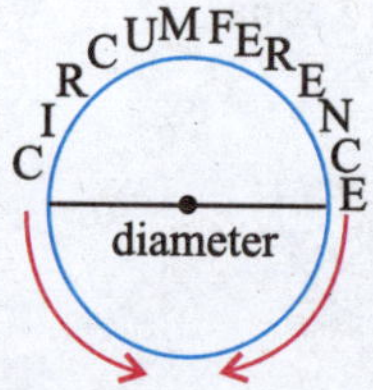

Segment

The region between a chord and either of its arcs is called a segment of the circular region or simply a segment of the circle. There are two segments, the **major segment** and the **minor segment.**

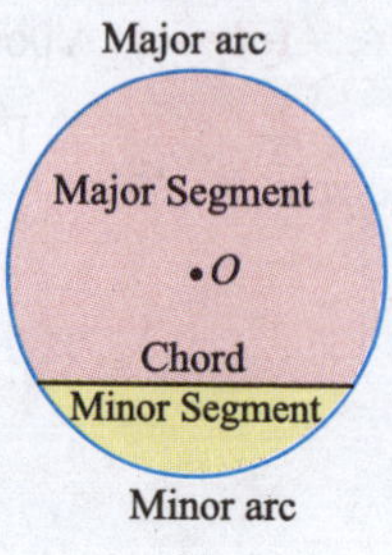

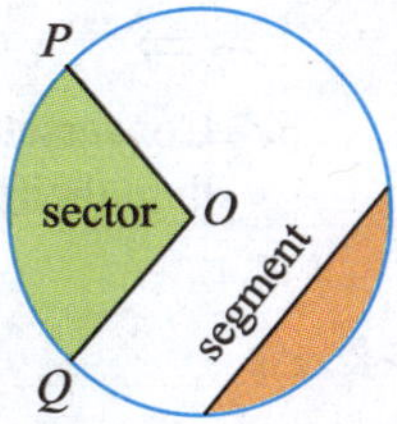

Sector : The region between an arc and the two radii, joining the centre to the end points is called a sector. Like segments, the minor arc corresponds to the minor sector and the major arc corresponds to the major sector. In Fig. the region *OPQ* is the minor sector and remaining part of the circular region is the major sector.

Note: When two arcs are equal, that is, each is a semicircle, then both segments and both sectors become the same.

1. Circles having same centre are said to be concentric circles.

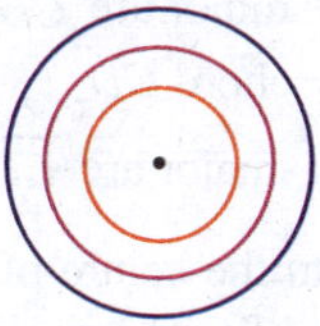

2. Two circles are congruent if and only if they have equal radii.

$OA = O'B$

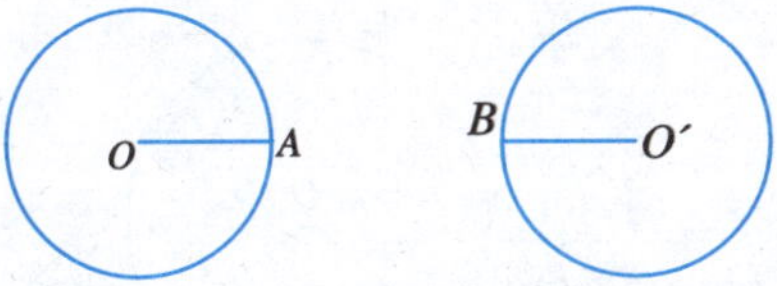

3. Two arcs of a circle (or of congruent circles) are said to be congruent if and only if they have the same degree measure.

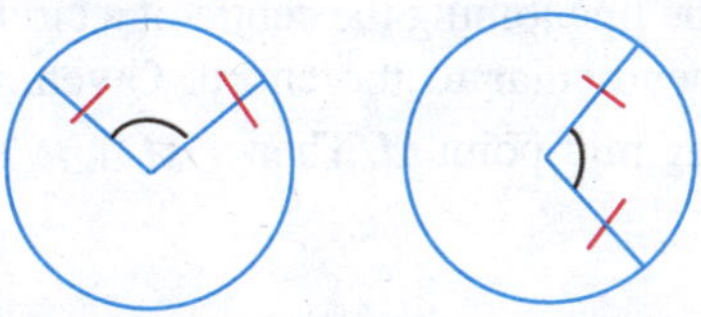

4. If two arcs of a circle (or of congruent circles) are congruent, then the corresponding chords are equal.

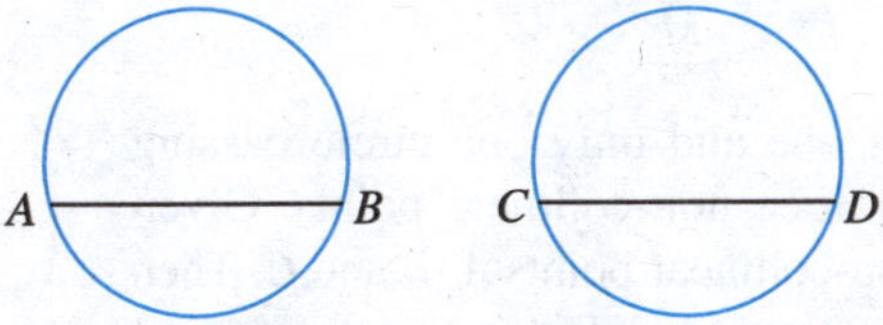

(i) **Minor arc** $\overparen{AB} \cong$ minor arc $\overparen{CD}$

$\Rightarrow$ chord AB = chord CD.

(ii) **Major arc** $\overparen{AB} \cong$ major arc $\overparen{CD}$

$\Rightarrow$ chord AB = chord CD

5. Conversely, if two chords of a circle (or of congruent circles) are equal, then their corresponding arcs are equal.

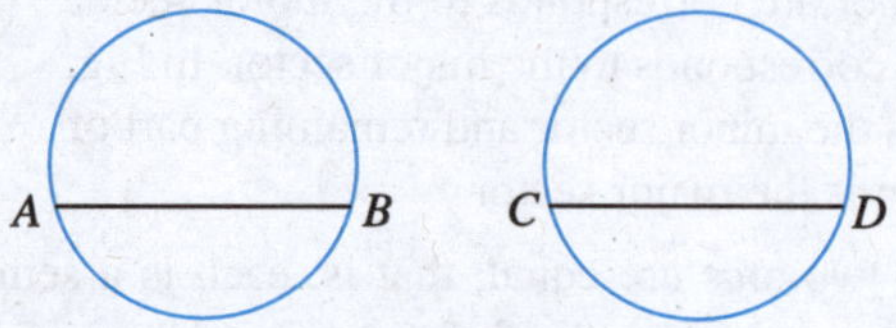

(i) chord AB = chord CD

$\Rightarrow$ Minor arc $\overparen{AB} \cong$ minor arc $\overparen{CD}$

(ii) chord AB = chord CD

$\Rightarrow$ Major arc $\overparen{AB} \cong$ major arc $\overparen{CD}$

6. The perpendicular from the centre of the circle to the chord bisects the chord. Given a chord PQ of a circle $C(O, r)$ and perpendicular OL drawn to the chord PQ. Then $PL = LQ$.

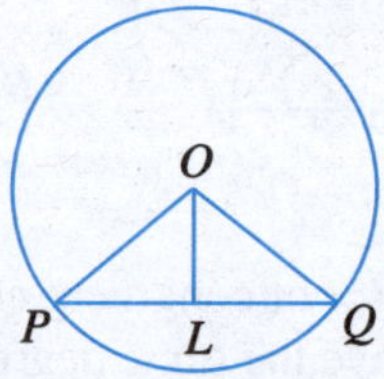

7. Conversely, the line joining the centre of a circle to the mid point of a chord is perpendicular to the chord. Given, chord PQ of a circle $C(O, r)$ having mid-point M. Then $OM \perp PQ$.

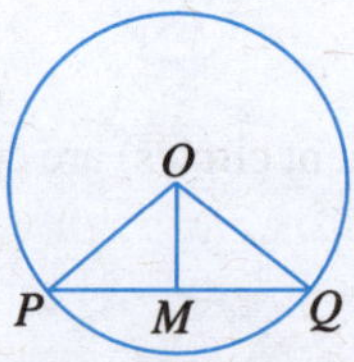

8. There is one and only one circle passing through three non-collinear points. Given three non-collinear points A, B and C. Then there is one and only one circle passing through these points. This can be proved by drawing perpendicular bisectors of AB and BC.

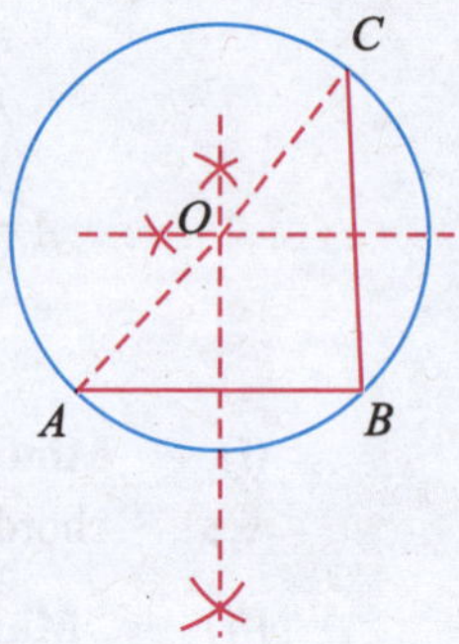

9. Equal chords of a circle (or of congruent circles) subtend equal angles at the centre (or corresponding centres).

A circle C (O, r) is given having two of its chords equal, *i.e.*, $AB = CD$. Then,

$\angle AOB = \angle COD$. Similarly, AB and CD are equal chords of two congruent circles C (O, r) and C (O', r) respectively.

Then $\angle AOB = \angle CO'D$.

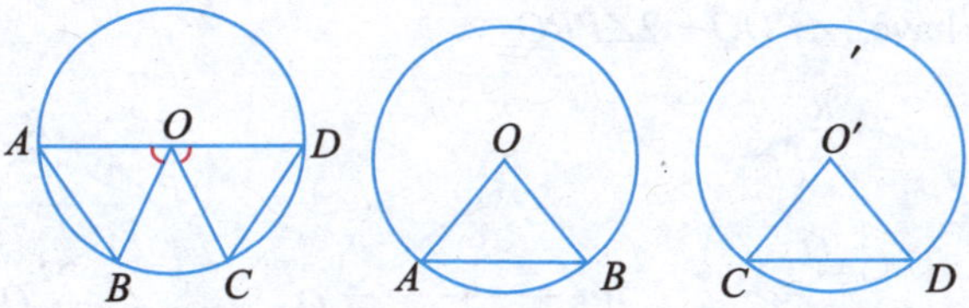

10. Conversely, if the angles subtended by two chords of a circle (or of congruent circles) at the centre (or at the corresponding centres) are equal, the chords are equal.

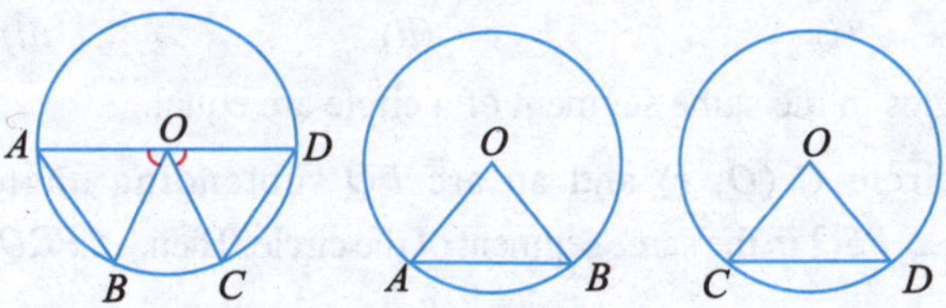

(a) (b) (c)

In circle c (O,r) in fig (a) $\angle AOB = \angle COD \Rightarrow$ chord AB = chord CD

In another two circle c (O, r) and c (O', r); in fig (b) and (c) respectively

$\angle AOB = \angle CO'D \Rightarrow$ chord AB = chord CD.

11. Equal chords of a circle (or of congruent circles) are equidistant from the centre (or corresponding centres).

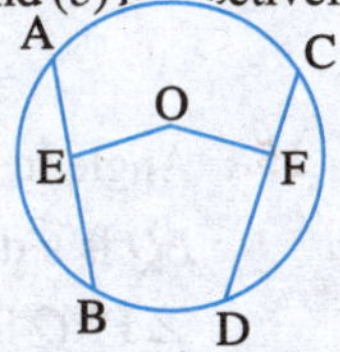

If Chord AB = chord CD, then

$OE = OF$

12. Chords of a circle which are equidistant from the centre are equal.

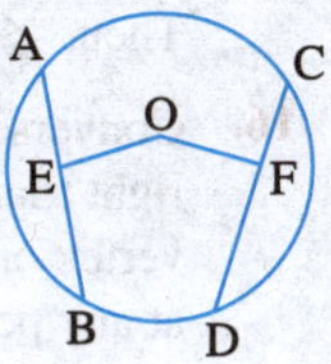

If $OE = OF$, then

Chord AB = chord CD

13. The degree measure of an arc of a circle at the centre is twice the angle subtended by it at any point of the alternate segment of the circle with respect to the arc.

An arc PQ of a circle $C(O, r)$ and a point R in the arc QP are given. Then, we have the following three cases:

(*a*) When $\overset{\frown}{PQ}$ is a minor arc (fig (*i*))

(*b*) When $\overset{\frown}{PQ}$ is a semi circle (fig (*ii*))

(*c*) When $\overset{\frown}{PQ}$ is a major arc (fig (*iii*))

We have, $\angle POQ = 2\angle PRQ$

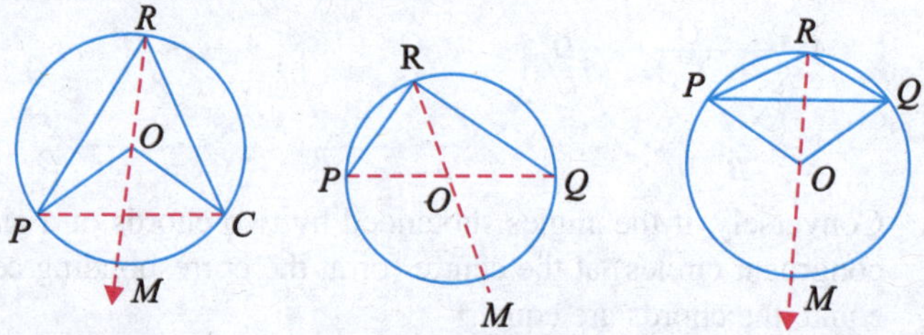

(*i*) (*ii*) (*iii*)

14. Angles in the same segment of a circle are equal.

A circle $C(O, r)$ and an arc PQ subtending angles $\angle PRQ$ and $\angle PSQ$ in the same segment of the circle. Then, $\angle PRQ = \angle PSQ$.

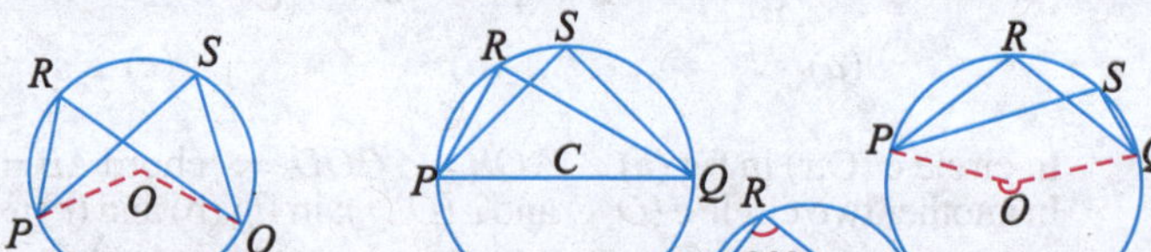

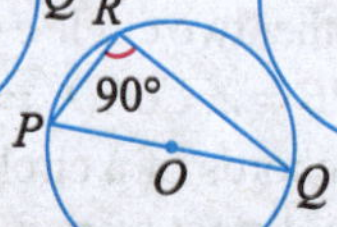

15. Angle in a semicircle is a right angle.

PQ is a diameter of a circle and

$\angle PRQ$ is an angle in semi-circle.

Then, $\angle PRQ = 90^0$.

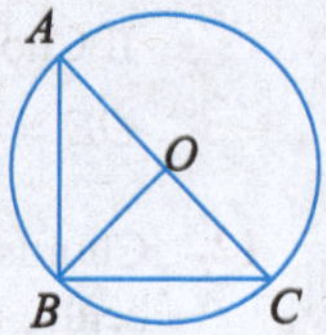

16. Conversely, the circle drawn with hypotenuse of a right triangle as diameter passes through its opposite vertex or the arc of a circle subtending a right angle at any point of the circle in its alternate segment is a semicircle.

17. If a line segment joining two points subtends equal angles at two other points lying on the same side of the line containing the segment, the four points lie on the same circle.

18. The sum of either pair of opposite angles of a cyclic quadrilateral is

180°.

ABCD is a cyclic quadrilateral, then $\angle A+\angle C=180^0$,

$\angle B+\angle D=180^0$

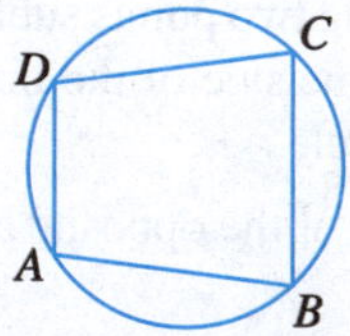

19. Conversely, if the sum of any pair of opposite angles of a quadrilateral is 180°, then the quadrilateral is cyclic.

20. If the side of a cyclic quadrilateral be produced, then the exterior angle so formed is equal to the opposite interior angle. Given, a cyclic quadrilateral *ABCD* whose side *AB* is produced to a point *E*. Then, $\angle CBE = \angle ADC$.

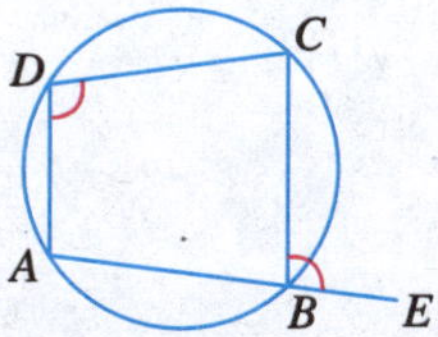

POINTS TO REMEMBER

1. Two circles are congruent if and only if they have equal radii.
2. Equal chords of a circle subtend equal angles at the centre and conversely, if the angles subtended by the chords at the centre (of a circle) are equal, then the chords are equal.
3. Two arcs of a circle are congruent if the angles subtended by them at the centre are equal and so its converse.
4. If two arcs of a circle are congruent, their corresponding chords are equal and so its converse.
5. The perpendicular from the centre of a circle to a chord bisects the chord and conversely, the line drawn through the centre of a circle to bisect a chord is perpendicular to the chord.
6. There is one and only one circle passing through three given non-collinear points.
7. Equal chords of a circle (or of congruent circles) are equidistant from the centre(s) and conversely, chords of a circle (or of congruent circles) that are equidistant from the centre(s) are equal.
8. The angle subtended by an arc at the centre is double the angle

subtended by it at any point on the remaining part of the circle.

9. The angle in a semicircle is a right angle and so its converse.
10. Angles in the same segment of a circle are equal.
11. If a line segment joining two points subtends equal angles at two other points lying on the same side of the line containing the segment, the four points lie on a circle.
12. The sum of either pair of the opposite angles of a cyclic quadrilateral is 180°.
13. If a pair of opposite angles of a quadrilateral is supplementary, then the quadrilateral is cyclic.

CHAPTER 11

CONSTRUCTIONS

Basic Constructions

Construction	Steps of construction	Figure
1. To construct the bisector of a given angle.	**1.** Taking B as centre and of any radius, draw an arc to intersect the rays BA and BC, at E and D respectively [see Fig.(i)]. **2.** Next, taking D and E as centers and with the radius more than DE, draw arcs to intersect each other, say at F. **3.** Draw the ray BF [see Fig.(*ii*)]. This ray BF is the required bisector of the angle ABC.	Fig. (*i*) 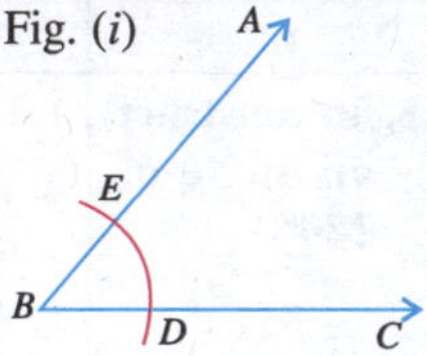 Fig. (*ii*) 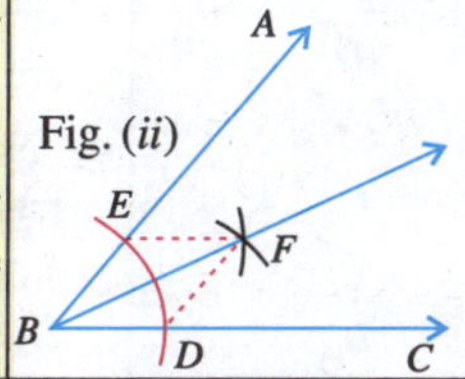
2. To construct the perpendicular bisector of a given line segment.	**1.** Taking A and B as centres and radius more than $\frac{1}{2}AB$, draw arcs on both sides of the line segment AB (to intersect each other). **2.** Let these arcs intersect each other at P and Q. Join PQ [see fig]. **3.** Let PQ intersect AB at the point M. Then line PMQ is the required perpendicular bisector of AB.	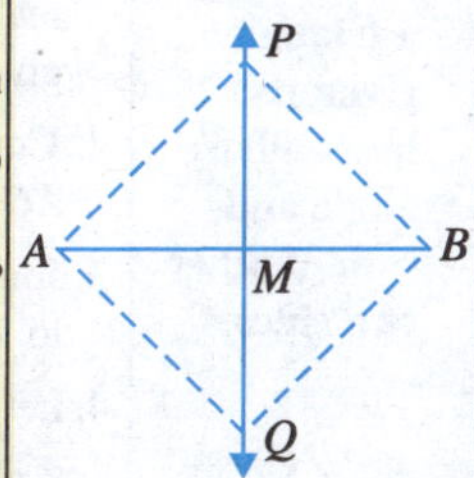
3. To construct an angle of 30° and 15°.	**1.** Draw any ray $\overrightarrow{OP}$. **2.** With O as centre and any convenient radius, draw an arc cutting OP at A. **3.** With A as centre and the same radius as in step 2 draw an arc to cut the previous arc at B. **4.** Join OB and produce it to form the ray OQ. Then $\angle POQ = 60°$. **5.** Bisect the angle $\angle POQ$ at C $\Rightarrow$ $\angle POC' = 30°$ $\angle POC'$ at D $\Rightarrow$ $\angle POD' = 15°$	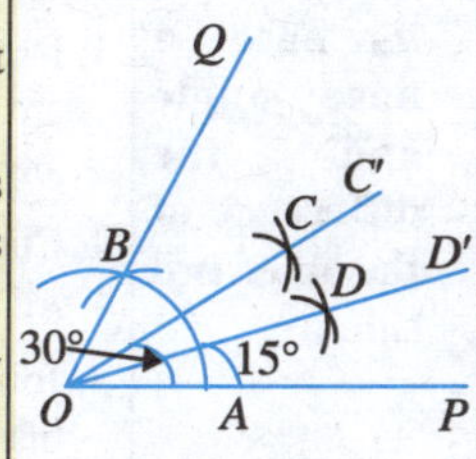

Construction	Steps of construction	Figure
4. To construct an angle of 60⁰ at the initial point of a given ray.	1. Taking A as centre and of any radius, draw an arc of a circle, which intersects AB, say at a point D. 2. Taking D as centre and with the same radius as before, draw an arc intersecting the previously drawn arc, say at a point E. 3. Draw the ray AC passing through E [see Fig (*ii*)]. Then $\angle CAB$ is the required angle of 60°.	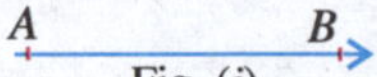 Fig. (*i*) 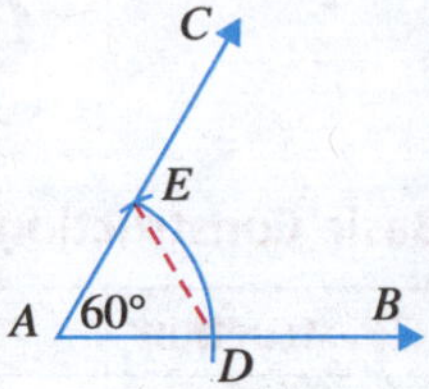 Fig. (*ii*)
5. To construct an angle of 120°.	1. Draw any ray OP. 2. With O as centre and any convenient radius, draw an arc cutting OP at A. 3. With A as centre and same radius as in step 2, draw an arc to cut the previous arc at B. 4. Now, with B as centre and the same radius, cut off the previous arc at B'. 5. Join OB' and produce it to form the ray OQ. Then, $\angle POQ = 120°$.	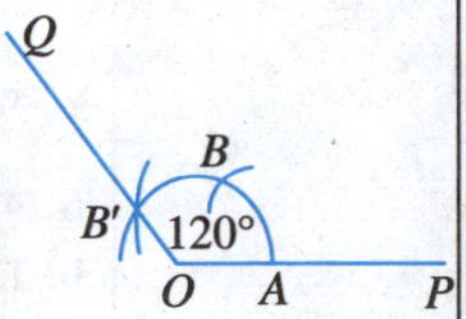
6. To construct a triangle, given its base, a base angle and sum of other two sides.	1. Draw the base BC and at the point B make an angle, say $\angle XBC$ equal to the given angle. 2. Cut a line segment BD equal to $AB + AC$ from the ray BX. 3. Join DC and make an angle DCY equal to $\angle BDC$. 4. Let CY intersect BX at A (see Fig.).Then, $\angle ABC$ is the required triangle.	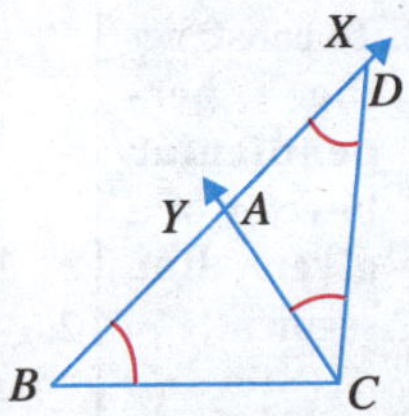
7. To construct a triangle given its base, a base angle and the difference of the other two sides.	**Case (*i*) : Let $AB > AC$ that is $AB - AC$ is given.** 1. Draw the base BC and at point B make an angle, say $\angle XBC$ equal to the given angle. 2. Cut the line segment BD equal to $AB - AC$ from ray BX. 3. Join DC and draw the perpendicular bisector, say PQ of DC. 4. Let it intersect BX at a point A. Join AC (see Fig.).Then ΔABC is the required triangle.	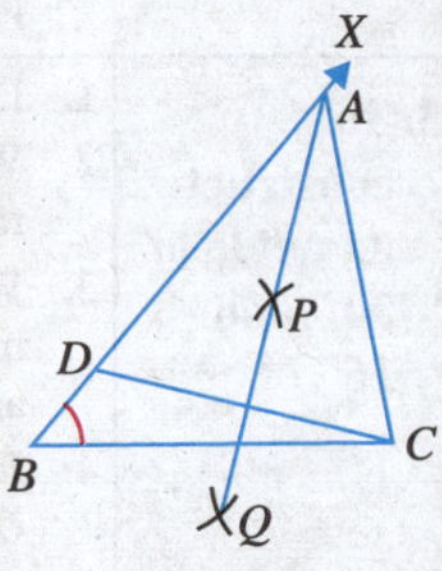

<table>
<tr><th>Construction</th><th>Steps of construction</th><th>Figure</th></tr>
<tr><td></td><td>

Case (*ii*) : Let $AB < AC$ that is $AC - AB$ is given.Steps of Construction :

1. Same as in case (*i*).
2. Cut line segment BD equal to $AC - AB$ from the line BX extended on opposite side of line segmentBC.
3. Join DC and draw the perpendicular bisector, say PQ of DC.
4. Let PQ intersect BX at A. Join AC (see Fig.).Then, ΔABC is the required triangle

</td><td>

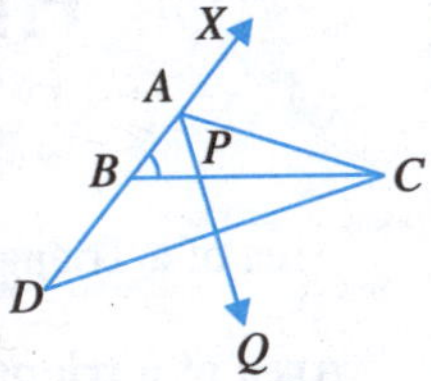

</td></tr>
<tr><td>

8. To construct a triangle, given its perimeter and its two base angles.

</td><td>

1. Draw a line segment, say XY equal to $BC + CA + AB$.
2. Make angles LXY equal to $\angle B$ and MYX equal to $\angle C$.
3. Bisect $\angle LXY$ and $\angle MYX$. Let these bisectors intersect at a point A [see Fig. (i)].
4. Draw perpendicular bisectors PQ of AX and RS of AY.
5. Let PQ intersect XY at B and RS intersect XY at C. Join AB and AC [see Fig (ii)].Then ABC is the required triangle.

</td><td>

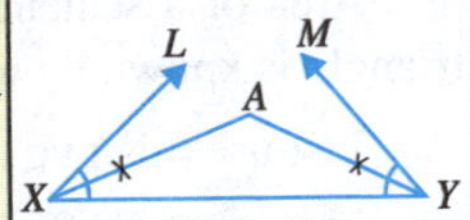

Fig. (*i*)

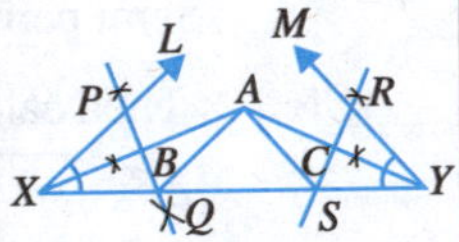

Fig. (*ii*)

</td></tr>
</table>

POINTS TO REMEMBER

1. Equal arcs cut off equal chords in equal circles or in the same circle.
2. If two isosceles triangles stand on opposite sides of the same base, the line joining their vertices, bisects the base at right-angles.
3. Any point on the perpendicular bisector of the join of two points is equidistance from two given points.
4. Equilateral triangle is equiangular, each of its angles being of 60°.
5. Every point lying in the right bisector of a straight line is equidistant from its extremities.
6. The angle in a semicircle is a right angle.
7. The exterior angle of a triangle is equal to the sum of the interior opposite angles.
8. If a transversal intersects two parallel lines, it makes :
   (*i*) Each pair of alternate angles equal and
   (*ii*) Each pair of corresponding angles equal.
9. The altitude of an isosceles triangle, bisects the vertical angle and also the base at right angles.
10. The side opposite to the right-angled triangle, is called the hypotenuse.

CHAPTER 12

HERON'S FORMULA

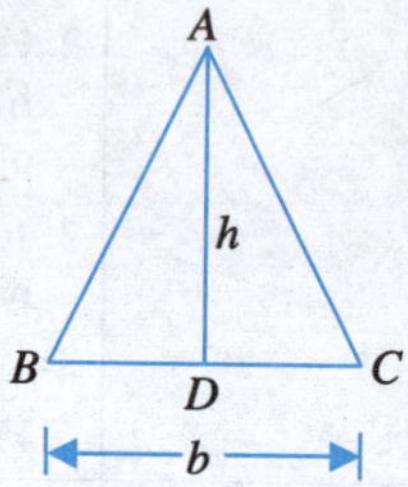

Area of a Triangle from sides

Area of a triangle = $\frac{1}{2} \times$ **Base** $\times$ **Height(altitude)**

$$= \frac{1}{2}bh$$

Area of a scalene triangle is calculated if length of all three sides of a triangle is known by using "Heron's Formula" after hero of Alexandria.

Just use this two step process:

Step 1: Calculate "s" (half of the triangles perimeter) using

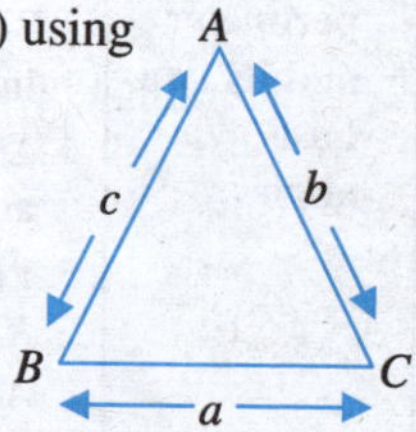

Semi perimeter, $s = \frac{a+b+c}{2}$

Step 2: Then calculate the Area using:

$$A = \sqrt{s(s-a)(s-b)(s-c)}$$

Area

Area of plane figure is the measure of region enclosed by it.

Unit of Area

Area of plane figure is two dimensional (length, breadth), therefore, area is measured in square units such as square cm (cm^2 or sq. cm.), square m (m^2 or sq. m), hectare (h m^2), *etc.*

Perimeter

Perimetre of a plane figure is the measure of the length of its boundary.

Unit of Perimeter

Perimeter has one dimension, i.e., it is the sum of lengths of boundary.

Therefore, unit of perimeter is same as unit of length i.e., centimetre (cm), metre (m), kilometre (km).

Isosceles Triangle

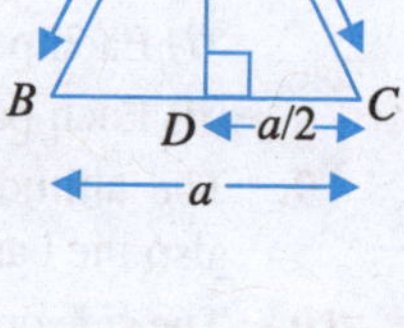

Let $AB = AC = b$. Base $BC = a$

Area $= \frac{1}{2} \times a \times \frac{\sqrt{4b^2 - a^2}}{2} = \frac{a\sqrt{4b^2 - a^2}}{4}$

Perimetre = $2b + a$

Right-Angled Triangle

Let b be the base, p be the perpendicular (height), and h be the hypotenuse, then

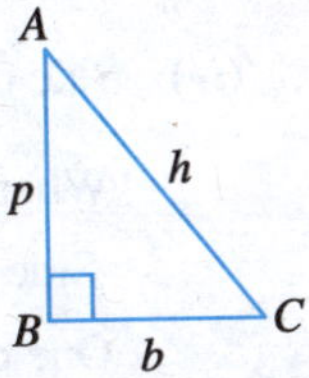

Hypotenuse $h = \sqrt{b^2 + p^2}$

Perimeter $= p + b + h$

Isosceles Right-Angled Triangle

Isosceles right angle triangle, right-angled at B and AB = BC = a

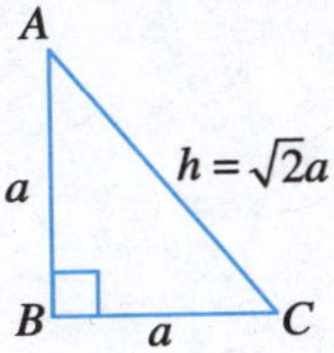

$$\text{Area} = \frac{1}{2} \times a \times a = \frac{a^2}{2}$$

Perimeter $= 2a + \sqrt{2}a$

Equilateral Triangle

$AB = BC = AC = a$ and height $= \frac{\sqrt{3}}{2}a$

$\angle A = \angle B = \angle C = 60°$

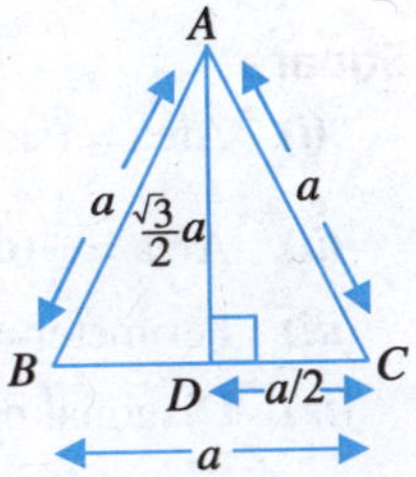

$$\text{Area} = \frac{1}{2} \times base \times height$$

$$= \frac{\sqrt{3}}{4}a^2$$

Perimeter = 3*a*

Rectangle (length *l* and breadth *b*)

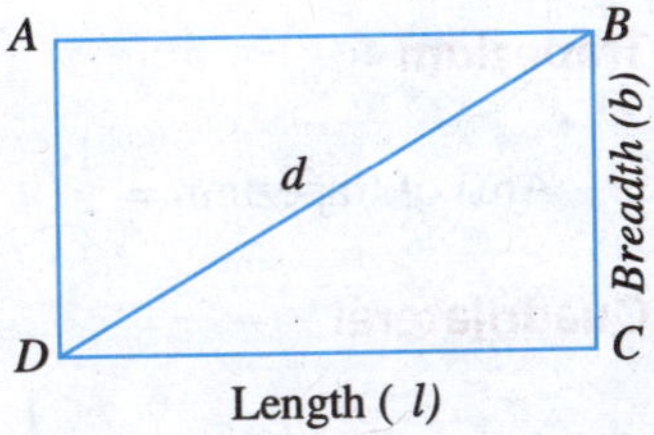

(*i*) Area = $l \times$ b

(*ii*) Diagonal = $\sqrt{l^2 + b^2}$

(*iii*) Perimeter = 2 (l + b)

Parallelogram

(*i*) Area = Base × Corresponding height = ah

(*ii*) Perimeter = 2 (a + b) units

(*iii*) Area of the parallelogram

$$= 2\sqrt{s(s-a)(s-b)(s-c)}$$

Where , $s = \frac{a+b+c}{2}$

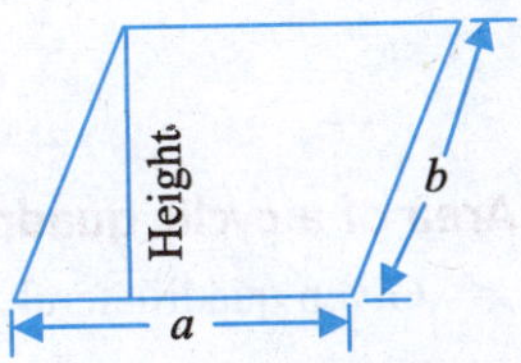

Rhombus

(*i*) Area of rhombus = $\frac{1}{2}d_1 \times d_2$

(*ii*) perimeter of rhombus = $2\sqrt{d_1^2 + d_2^2}$

(*iv*) Side of rhombus = $\frac{1}{2}\sqrt{d_1^2+d_2^2}$

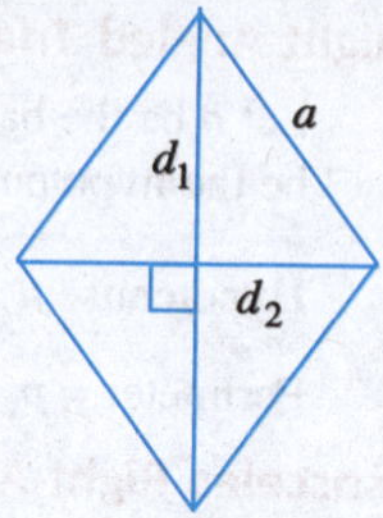

When one side and one diagonal are given

Side = a

One diagonal = d_1

$$\text{Other diagonal} = \sqrt{a^2-\frac{d_1^2}{4}}$$

$$=\frac{1}{2}\sqrt{4a^2-d_1^2}$$

$$\text{Area} = \frac{1}{2}\times d_1\times\frac{1}{2}\sqrt{4a^2-d_1^2}$$

$$=\frac{1}{4}\times d_1\sqrt{4a^2-d_1^2}$$

Square

(*i*) Area = (side)^2 = a^2

(*ii*) Area = $\frac{1}{2}$(diagonal)^2

(*iii*) Perimeter = 4a units

(*iv*) Diagonal of square = $\sqrt{2}\,a$ units

(*v*) Side of square = $\sqrt{\text{Area}} = \frac{\text{Perimeter}}{4}$

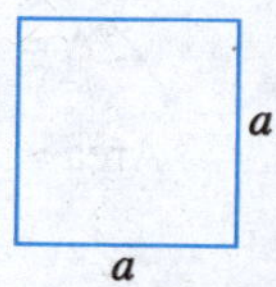

Trapezium

Area of trapezium = $\frac{1}{2}(a+b)\times h$

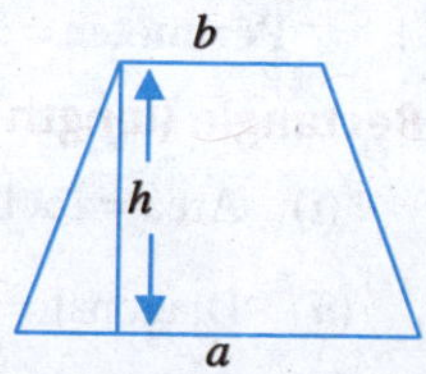

Quadrilateral

Area of quadrilateral = $\frac{1}{2}\times AC\times(h_1+h_2)$

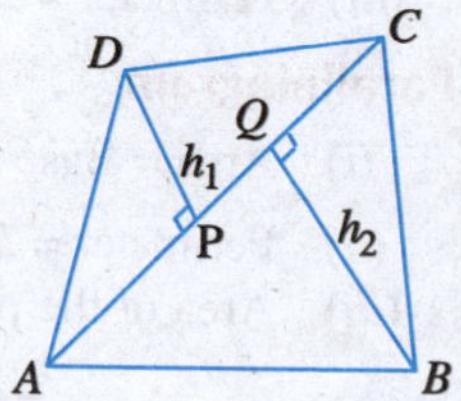

Area of a cyclic quadrilateral

Given quadrilateral ABCD with sides measuring a,b,c,d.

Area = $\sqrt{(s-a)(s-b)(s-c)(s-d)}$

Where $s=\frac{a+b+c+d}{2}$

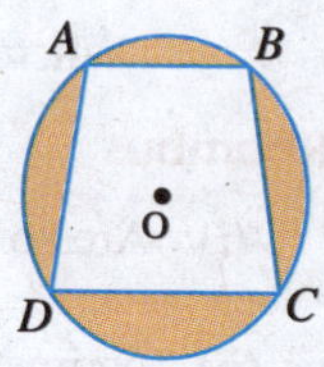

CHAPTER 13

SURFACE AREAS AND VOLUMES

UNITS OF MEASUREMENT OF AREA AND VOLUME

LENGTH

1 cm = 10 mm

1 dm = 10 cm

1 m = 10 dm

1 m = 100 cm

1 m = 1000 mm

1 decameter (dm) = 10 m

1 hm = 10 dm = 100 m

1 km = 1000 m = 100 dm = 10 hm

AREA

1 cm^2 = 100 mm^2

1 dm^2 = 100 cm^2

1 m^2 = 100 dm^2

1 dm^2 or 1 are = 100 m^2

1 hm^2 = 1 hectare = 10000 m^2 = 100 dm^2

1 km^2 = 100 hm^2 = 100 hectare

VOLUME

1 cm^3 = 1 ml = 1000 mm^3

1 l = 1000 ml = 1000 cm^3

1 m^3 = 10^6 cm^3 = 1000 l = 1 kl

1 dm^3 = 1000 cm^3

1 m^3 = 1000 dm^3

1 km^3 = 10^9 m^3

Cuboid

(i) Volume of a cuboid = lbh

(ii) Total surface area of a cuboid = $2(lb + bh + hl)$.

(iii) Lateral surface area of a cuboid = $2h(l + b)$.

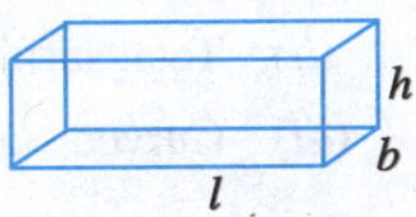

(*iv*) Diagonal of a cuboid = $\sqrt{l^2+b^2+h^2}$

(*v*) Area of four walls of a room = $2(l+b)h$

= **(perimeter of the floor)** × height

Cube

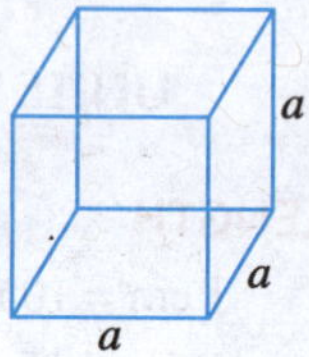

(*i*) Volume of a cube = a^3

(*ii*) Total surface area of a cube = $6a^2$

(*iii*) Lateral surface area of a cube = $4a^2$

(*iv*) Diagonal of a cube = $\sqrt{3}a$

Cylinder

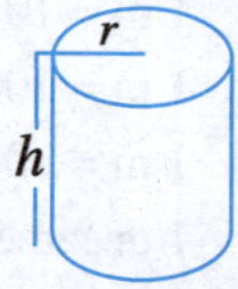

(*i*) Volume of a cylinder $= \pi r^2 h$

= (Area of the base) × Height

(*ii*) Total surface area of a cylinder $= (2\pi rh + 2\pi r^2)$

$= 2\pi r\,(r + h)$

(*iii*) Curved surface area of a cylinder $= 2\pi rh$

= (Perimeter of the base) × Height

(*iv*) Area of each end or Base area $= \pi r^2$

Hollow Cylinders

(*i*) Volume of the material

= (Exterior volume) – (Interior volume)

$= (\pi R^2 h - \pi r^2 h) = \pi h(R^2 - r^2)$

(*ii*) Curved surface of the hollow cylinder

= [(External surface) + (Internal surface)]

$= (2\pi Rh + 2\pi rh) = [2\pi h(R+r)]$

(*iii*) Total surface area of the hollow cylinder

= Curved surface + 2 (Area of base ring)

$= (2\pi Rh + 2\pi rh) + 2(\pi R^2 - \pi r^2)$

$= [(2\pi h(R+r) + 2\pi(R^2 - r^2)]$

$= [2\pi(R+r)(h+R-r)]$

Cone

(*i*) Volume of a cone $= \frac{1}{3}\pi r^2 h$

(*ii*) Total surface area of cone $= \pi r\,(l + r)$

(*iii*) Curved surface area of cone $= \pi rl$

$= \pi r\sqrt{r^2+h^2}$

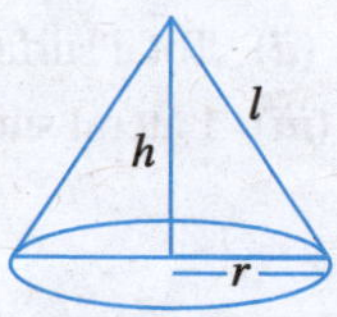

(*iv*) Slant height of a cone $l = \sqrt{h^2+r^2}$

Sphere

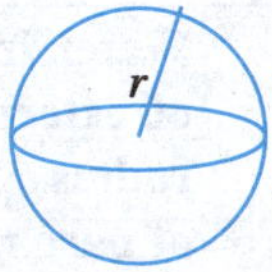

(i) Volume of a sphere = $\frac{4}{3}\pi r^3$

(ii) Total surface area of sphere = $4\pi r^2$

Hemisphere

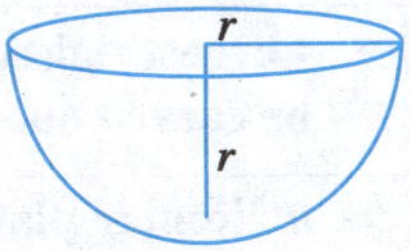

(i) Volume of a hemisphere = $\frac{2}{3}\pi r^3$

(ii) Total surface area of a hemisphere = $3\pi r^2$

(iii) Curved surface area of a hemisphere = $2\pi r^2$

Conversions of Solids:

Conversion of solid	Formulae
A metallic sphere or ball of radius '*R*' melted and recast into n smaller spherical balls of radius '*r*'.	$\frac{4}{3}\pi R^3 = n \times \frac{4}{3}\pi r^3$ or $n = \frac{R^3}{r^3}$
A metallic sphere or ball of radius '*R*' melted and recast into a long wire of radius '*r*' and length '*h*'.	$\frac{4}{3}\pi R^3 = \pi r^2 h$
A metallic spherical shell of external radius 'r_2' and internal radius 'r_1' is melted and recast into n smaller spherical balls of radius '*r*'.	$\frac{4}{3}\pi (r_2^3 - r_1^3) = n \times \frac{4}{3}\pi r^3$
A metallic cone of radius '*R*' and height 'h' is melted and recast into n balls each of radius '*r*'.	$\frac{1}{3}\pi R^2 h = n \times \frac{4}{3}\pi r^3$
A metallic spherical shell of external radius 'r_2' and internal radius 'r_1' is melted and recast into a solid circular cylinder of height '*h*' and radius '*r*'.	$\frac{4}{3}\pi (r_2^3 - r_1^3) = \pi r^2 h$
A metallic ball of radius 'R' is melted and recast into 3 spherical balls of radii 'r_1', 'r_2' and 'r_3'.	$\frac{4}{3}\pi R^3 = \frac{4}{3}\pi r_1^3 + \frac{4}{3}\pi r_2^3 + \frac{4}{3}\pi r_3^3$
A spherical ball of radius '*R*' is dropped into a cylindrical vessel of base radius '*r*' partly filled with water.	Let the rise in level of water by 'h'. Then, $\frac{4}{3}\pi R^3 = \pi r^2 h$

Water from a hemispherical shell of external radius r_2 and internal radius r_1 is transferred to n bottles of base radius '*r*' and height '*h*'.	$\frac{2}{3}\pi(r_2^3 - r_1^3) = n \times \pi r^2 h$
Largest sphere carved out of a cube of side '*a*'.	Diameter of sphere, $2r$ = side/edge of the cube. $r = a/2$
Largest right circular cone that can be carved out of a cube of edge '*a*'.	Diameter of base of cone, $2r$ = side/edge of the cube. $r = a/2$
***n* circular plates or coins of radius '*r*' and thickness '*h*' are placed one above the other to form a solid right circular cylinder.**	Height of cylinder = nh Volume of '*n*' plates $= n \times \pi r^2 h$ Total Surface area $= 2\pi r(r + nh)$

CHAPTER 14

STATISTICS

Data

Facts or figures, which are numerical or otherwise, collected with a definite purpose are called the *data*.

Data is the plural form of the Latin word *datum*.

Statistics

Statistics is the science that deals with collection, organization, analysis and interpretation of data.

Collection of Data

When some information is collected by the investigator, with a definite objective, the data thus obtained is called the **primary data**.

When information is gathered from the source which already had the information stored, the data obtained is called the **secondary data**. Such data, which has been collected by someone else in another context, needs to be used with great care ensuring that the source is reliable.

Presentation of Data

As soon as the work related to collection of data is over, the investigator has to find out ways to present them in a form which is meaningful, easily understood and gives its main features at a glance.

Raw or ungrouped data

The data obtained in the original form are called raw data.

Range

The difference of the highest and the lowest values in the data is called the *range* of the data.

Grouped data

When data is condensed into classes or groups, we call it grouped data.

Frequency of an observation

The number of times an observation occurs is called its frequency.

Frequency distribution of an ungrouped data

The tabular arrangement of data showing the frequency of each observation is called a frequency distribution.

Tally marks

We use these tally marks /, //, ///, *etc.*, for counting.

Class interval

Each group into which the raw data is condensed is called a class interval

Classes or Class Intervals

Score	Number of Innings
0 – 9	12
10 – 19	9
20 – 29	6
30 – 39	8
40 – 49	10
	Total Innings = 45

Class size

The difference between the true upper limit and the true lower limit is called its class size.

Class mark

It is equal to $\dfrac{\text{Upper class limit + Lower class limit}}{2}$

Method of forming classes of a data:

1. Determine the maximum and minimum values of the variate occurring in the data.
2. Decide upon the number of classes to be formed.
3. Find the range, *i.e.*, the difference between the maximum value and the minimum value.
4. Divide the range by the number of classes to be formed.
5. Count and obtain the frequency of each class and tabulate it.

Cumulative frequency

The Cumulative frequency corresponding to a class is the sum of all frequencies up to and including that class.

Cumulative frequency distribution table

A table showing the cumulative frequencies over various classes is called a Cumulative frequency distribution table.

Graphical Representation of Data

We shall study the following graphical representations in this section.

(A) Bar graphs

(B) Histograms of uniform width, and of varying widths

(C) Frequency polygons

(A) Bar Graphs

A bar graph is a pictorial representation of data in which usually bars of uniform width are drawn with equal spacing between them on one axis (say, the *x*-axis), depicting the variable. The values of the variables are shown on the other axis (say, the *y*-axis) and the heights of the bars depend on the values of the variable.

(B) Histogram

This is a form of representation like the bar graph, but it is used for continuous class intervals. Since there are no gaps in between consecutive rectangles, the resultant graph appears like a solid figure. This is called a *histogram*, which is a graphical representation of a grouped frequency distribution with continuous classes.

For Example : Draw a histogram to represent the following data for the earning of workers

Monthly earnings (in rupees)	No. of workers
80 – 120	4
120 – 160	7
160 – 200	13
200 – 240	8
240 – 280	5
280 – 320	2

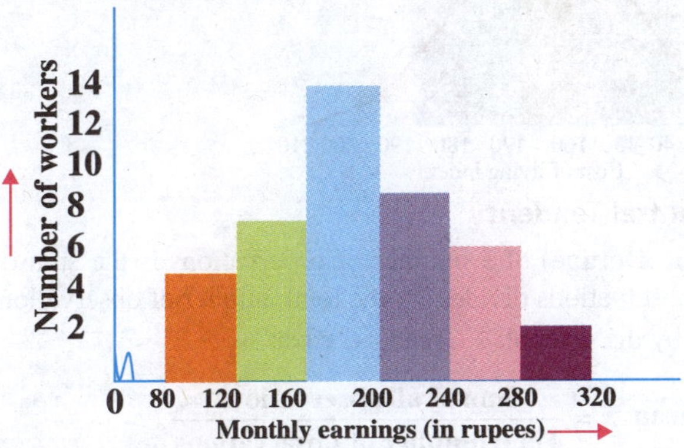

(C) Frequency Polygon

There is yet another visual way of representing quantitative data and its frequencies.

This is a polygon. Let us join the mid-points of the upper sides of the adjacent rectangles of a histogram by means of line segments. Let us call these mid-points *B*, *C*, *D*, *E*, *F* and *G*. When joined by line segments, we obtain the figure *BCDEFG*. *Frequency polygons can also be drawn independently without drawing histograms.* For this, we require the mid-points of the class-intervals used in the data. These mid-points of the class-intervals are called **class-marks**.

Example : In a city the following weekly observations were made in a study on cost of living index for the Year 2009-10

Cost of living index	Number of week
140 – 150	5
150 – 160	10
160 – 170	20
170 – 180	9
180 – 190	6
190 – 200	2
Total	**52**

Draw a histogram and a frequency polygon, on the same scale.

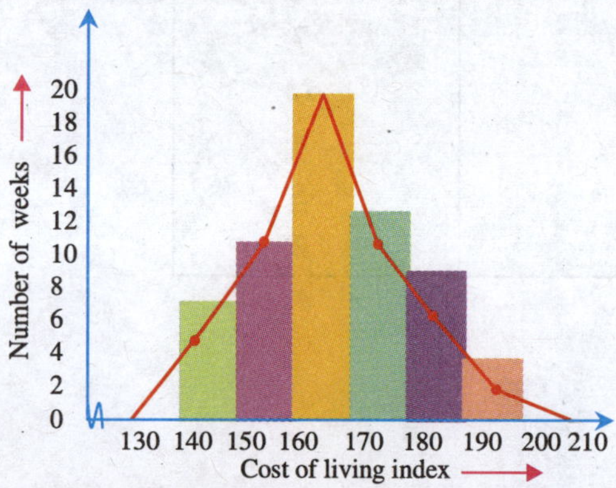

Measures of Central Tendency

The **mean** (or **average**) of a number of observations is the sum of the values of all the observations divided by the total number of observations.

It is denoted by the symbol $\bar{x}$, read as 'x bar'.

Therefore, **mean** $\bar{x} = \dfrac{\textbf{Sum of all observations}}{\textbf{Total number of observations}}$

Mean of a given set of values is equal to the sum of all the values divided by the total number of values.

$$\bar{x} = \frac{\sum_{i=1}^{n} x_i}{n}$$

$\bar{x}$ = Mean

$\sum$ = Summation sign

n = Number of values

x_i = Values of x with i ranging from 1 to n

Ungrouped frequency distribution

Sum or Products of different values of X and their corresponding frequencies

Mean

$$\bar{x} = \frac{\sum_{i=1}^{n} f_i x_i}{\sum_{i=1}^{n} f_i}$$

Sum of all The frequencies of X

The **median** is that value of the given number of observations, which divides it into exactly two parts. So, when the data is arranged in ascending (or descending) order the median of ungrouped data is calculated as follows:

(i) When the number of observations (n) is odd, the median is the value of the $\left(\frac{n+1}{2}\right)^{th}$ observation.

For example, if $n = 13$, the value of the $\left(\frac{13+1}{2}\right)^{th}$ observation, i.e., the 7th observation will be the median.

(ii) When the number of observations (n) is even, the median is the mean of the $\left(\frac{n}{2}\right)^{th}$ and $\left(\frac{n}{2}+1\right)^{th}$ observations.

For example, if $n = 16$, the mean of the values of the $\left(\frac{16}{2}\right)^{th}$ and $\left(\frac{16}{2}+1\right)^{th}$ observations, *i.e.*, the mean of the values of the 8th and 9th observations will be the median.

Mode

The **mode** is that value of the observation which occurs most frequently, *i.e.*, an observation with the maximum frequency is called the mode.

Example: 10, 9, 11, 9, 10, 7, 88, 9, 11, 9, 9, 6.

Here the items of maximums frequency is 9 which occurs 5 times, which is the greatest of the frequencies of the other observations.

Therefore, Mode of the series is 9. Or in other words, the item which occurs **most** frequently in a data is called its mode.

Empirical Formula of Mode

In case, two or more items occur the same number of time, we use the following formula to determine the mode:

Mode = 3 Median – 2 Mean

CHAPTER 15

PROBABILITY

1. Probability

Probability is a measure of uncertainty. We deal with those situations in which a particular result or outcome is not certain, but it can be any one of the several possible outcomes.

(*a*) **Experimental or empirical probabilities:** The probabilities that are based on the results of actual experiments and adequate recordings of the happening of the events.

(*b*) **Theoretical or classical probability** of an event ***E*** **:**

$$P(E) = \frac{\textbf{Number of outcomes favourable to } E}{\textbf{Total Number of possible outcomes}}.$$

(*c*) **Experiment :** An operation which can produce some well-defined outcomes, is called an experiment.

(*d*) **Random Experiment :** An experiment which when performed produces one of the several possible outcomes is called a random experiment.

(*e*) **Trial :** By a trial, we mean performing a random experiment.

(*f*) **Event:** The outcome of an experiment is called an event.

(*g*) **Compound events :** A collection of two or more possible outcomes of an experiment is called a compound event.

(*h*) **Elementary event:** An event having only one outcome of the experiment is called an elementary event. The sum of the probabilities of all the elementary events of an experiment is 1.

(*i*) **Equally likely events:** If we can reasonably assume that each outcome of an elementary experiment is as likely to occur as the other, We refer to this by saying that the outcomes are equally likely. For example, the equally likely outcomes of throwing a die are 1, 2, 3, 4, 5 and 6.

(*j*) **Sample Space, S:** The set of all the events that could be associated with an experiment is called its Sample Space, denoted by *S*.

(*k*) **Probability of a sure event is 1 and probability of an impossible event is 0.** From the definition of the probability *P* (*E*), we see that the numerator (number of outcomes favourable to the event E) is always less than or equal to the denominator (the number of all possible outcomes).

Therefore, $0 \le p\,(E) \le 1$

(*l*) $P\,(E) + P\,(\text{Not } E) = 1$

['not E', is called the **complement** of the event E.]

(*m*) The sum of the probabilities of all the elementary events of an experiment is 1, i.e., $P(E_1) + P(E_2) + ... + P(E_n) = 1$

Event	Sample Space
A Coin is tossed	$S = \{H, T\}$
Two coins are tossed	$S = \{HH, HT, TH, TT\}$
Three coins are tossed	$S = \{HHH, HHT, HTH, HTT, THH, THT, TTH, TTT\}$
A die is thrown	$S = \{1, 2, 3, 4, 5, 6\}$
Two dice are thrown	$S = \{(1,1), (1,2), (1,3), (1,4), (1,5), (1,6), (2,1), (2,2), (2,3), \ldots, (6,1), (6,2), (6,3), (6,4), (6,5), (6,6)$
A card is drawn from deck of cards.	A deck of cards has 52 cards, 26 of black suit and 26 of red suit. Out of the 26 cards of black suit, 13 are of clubs and 13 of spades. Out of the 26 cards of red suit, 13 are of Hearts and 13 of diamonds. The cards in each suit are Ace, 2, 3, 4, 5, 6, 7, 8, 9, 10, Jack, Queen and King.
A bag containing p red, q blue and r green balls.	Total No. of balls $= p + q + r$.

Experiment

An experiment is an activity which ends in a well defined result. The probability of an event lies between 0 and 1 (both inclusive). If p is the probability of the occurrence of an event; then q, the probability of not occurrence is given by $q = 1 - p$

Sure event

If the probability of occurrence of an event is 1, it is called sure event.

Impossible event: If the probability of occurrence of an event is 0, it is called an impossible event.

Note: See page no 128 for coloured playing cards.

CHAPTER 1

REAL NUMBERS

Divisibility

A non-zero integer 'a' is said to divide an integer 'b' if there exists an integer c such that $b = ac$.

Euclid's Division Lemma

Let a and b be any two positive integers. Then, there exist unique integers q and r such that $a = bq + r$, $0 \leq r < b$.

The Euclid Division Lemma is a restatement of the long division process and the integers q and r are called the quotient and remainder respectively.

Application of Euclid's Division Lemma to compute HCF of two positive integers

1. Let the two numbers be a and b.
2. Apply Euclid's Division Lemma to a and b and obtain two whole numbers q_1 and r_1 such that $a = bq_1 + r_1, 0 \leq r_1 < b$.
3. If $r_1 = 0$, b is the HCF of a and b.
4. If $r_1 \neq 0$, apply Euclid's Division Lemma to b and r_1 and obtain two whole numbers q_1 and r_2 such that $b = q_1 r_1 + r_2$.
5. If $r_2 = 0$, then r_1 is the HCF of a and b.
6. If $r_2 \neq 0$, then apply Euclid's Division Lemma to r_1 and r_2 and continue the above steps till the remainder r_n becomes zero. The divisor at this stage is the HCF of a and b.

Note: Euclid's Division Algorithm can be extended for all integers except zero, *i.e.*, $b \neq 0$.

It is one of the earliest examples of an algorithm that a computer has been programmed to carry out.

The fundamental Theorem of Arithmetic

Every composite number can be written as the product of powers of primes and this factorization is unique, apart from the order in which the prime factors occur. Or, the prime factorization of a natural number is unique, except for the order of its factors.

Factor Tree

Let us look at the example given below.

We can factorize a very large number.

such as 32760.

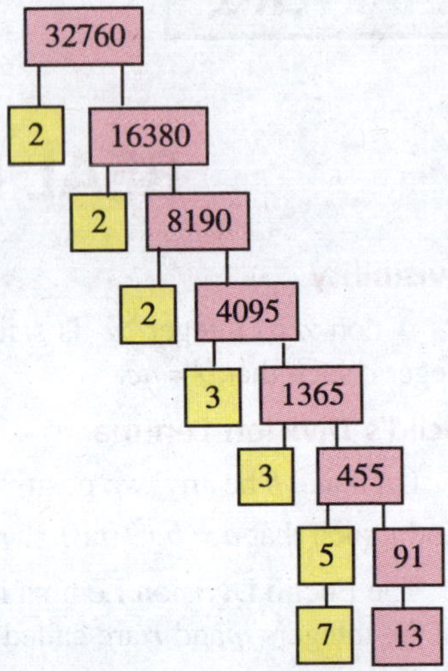

HCF and LCM by prime factorization method

The fundamental theorem of arithmetic can be used to find the HCF and LCM of two positive integers in the following way:

HCF = Product of the smallest power of each common prime factor in the numbers.

LCM = Product of the greatest power of each prime factor involved in the numbers.

For any two positive integers a and b, $\mathbf{HCF}(a, b) \times \mathbf{LCM}(a, b) = a \times b$.

Irrational Numbers

A number 's' is called irrational if it cannot be written in the form $\frac{p}{q}$, where p and q are integers and $q \neq 0$.

Examples of irrational numbers are: $\sqrt{2}, \sqrt{3}, \pi,$ 0.1033033303333..., *etc*.

The sum or difference of a rational and an irrational number is always irrational. The product and quotient of a non-zero rational and irrational number is irrational.

Theorem

Let p be a prime number. If p divides by a^2, then p divides by a, where a is a positive integer.

Decimal expansion of Rational Numbers

Let x be a rational number whose decimal expansion terminates, then x can be expressed in the form $\frac{p}{q}$, where p and q are coprime, and the prime factorization of q is of the form $2^n 5^m$, where n, m are non-negative integers.

Let $x = \frac{p}{q}$ be a rational number, such that the prime factorization of q is not of the form $2^n 5^m$, where n, m are non-negative integers. Then, x has a decimal expansion which is non-terminating repeating (recurring).

Example: Use Euclid's division algorithm to find the HCF of 210 and 55.

Solution: Since, $210 > 55$, we apply Euclid's division lemma to 210 and 55 and get $210 = 55 \times 3 + 45$.

Since the remainder $45 \neq 0$, we apply the division lemma to the divisor 55 and remainder 45 to get $55 = 45 \times 1 + 10$.

Since the remainder $10 \neq 0$, we apply the division lemma to the divisor 45 and new remainder 10 and get $45 = 10 \times 4 + 5$.

Since the remainder $5 \neq 0$, we apply the division lemma to the divisor 10 and new remainder 5 and get $10 = 5 \times 2 + 0$.

The remainder at this stage is zero and therefore, HCF of 210 and 55 is the divisor 5.

Revisiting Rational Numbers and their Decimal Expansions

Let us consider a rational number, say $\frac{p}{q}, q \neq 0$, and explore when the decimal expansion of $\frac{p}{q}$ is terminating and when it is non-terminating repeating.

Theorem:

1. Let x be a rational number whose decimal expansion terminates. Then x can be expressed in the form $\frac{p}{q}$, where p and q are coprime, and the prime factorisation of q is of the form $2^n 5^m$, where n, m are non-negative integers.

2. Let $x = \frac{p}{q}$ be a rational number, such that the prime factorization of q is of the form $2^n 5^m$, where n, m are non-negative integers. Then x has a decimal expansion which terminates.

3. Let $x = \dfrac{p}{q}$ be a rational number, such that the prime factorization of q is not of the form $2^n 5^m$, where n, m are non-negative integers. Then, x has a decimal expansion which is non-terminating repeating (recurring).

Conclusion

The decimal expansion of every rational number is either terminating or non-terminating repeating.

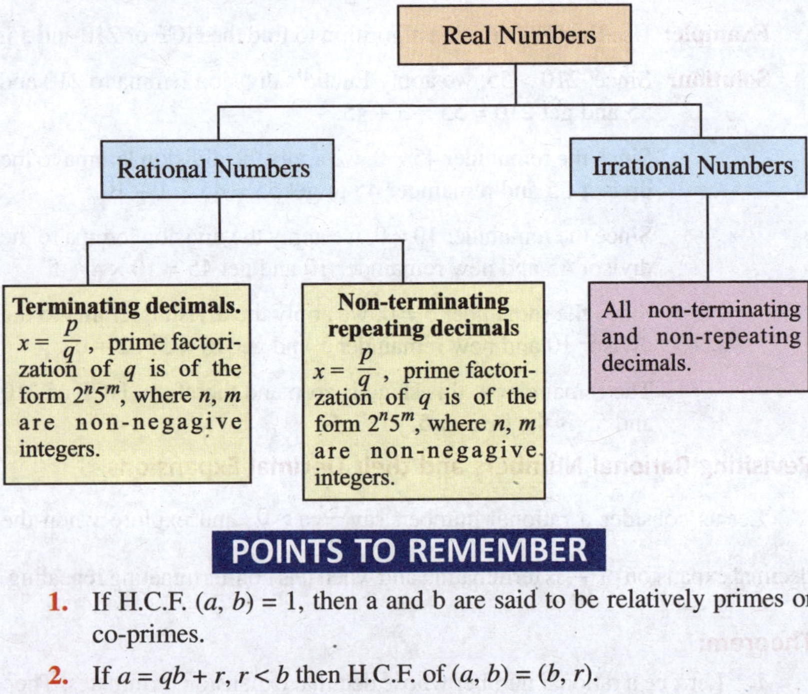

POINTS TO REMEMBER

1. If H.C.F. $(a, b) = 1$, then a and b are said to be relatively primes or co-primes.
2. If $a = qb + r$, $r < b$ then H.C.F. of $(a, b) = (b, r)$.
3. Euclid's algorithm is a technique of successive division used to find out H.C.F. of two or more numbers
4. If a, b, m are natural numbers, then H.C.F. of am, bm is m times H.C.F. of a and b or for all $a, b, m \in$ N, H.C.F $(am, bm) = m$ H.C.F. (a, b)
5. H.C.F. of there numbers is the H.C.F. of the H.C.F. of any two of them and the third numbers.
6. If H.C.F. of $(a, b) = 1$ and a is a factor of bc then a is a factor of c. This is known as Gauss's theorem.
7. The product of L.C.M. and H.C.F. of two numbers a and b is equal to the product of the numbers itself.

8. L.C.M. of two prime numbers or of two co-primes is equal to their product.

9. A rational number $\frac{a}{b}$ in lowest terms has a terminating decimal expression if and only if b has no prime factors other then 2 and 5.

10. A number which cannot be expressed as the ratio $\frac{a}{b}$, $a, b \in I, b \neq 0$ is called irrational number.

11. If α be an irrational number, then $-\alpha$ and $\frac{1}{\alpha}$ are also irrational.

12. If $\sqrt{ab}$ be an irrational number then $\sqrt{a}+\sqrt{b}$ is also irrational.

13. The decimal representation of an irrational number is always non-terminating, non-repeating.

14. If α be an irrational number and r a non-zero rational number, then the sum, difference, product and quotient of r and α are also irrational.

CHAPTER 2

POLYNOMIALS

Degree of a polynomial

If $p(x)$ is a polynomial in x, the highest power of x in $p(x)$ is called the **degree of the polynomial**.

For Example, $5x+10$ is a polynomial in variable x and is of degree 1.

$7-2y+3y^2$ is a polynomial in variable y and is of degree 2.

$3u^3+2u^2+\sqrt{5}$ is a polynomial in variable u and is of degree 3.

A polynomial of degree 1 is called a **linear polynomial**. Examples of linear polynomials are $3x+\frac{3}{5}, x-3y+1, \sqrt{3}u-\frac{2}{3}v+1$. The general form of a linear polynomial is $ax+b\ a\neq 0$ and a, b are real numbers.

A polynomial of degree 2 is called a **quadratic polynomial**. Examples of linear polynomials are $3x^2+\frac{3}{5}, y^2-3y+1, \sqrt{3}u^2-\frac{2}{3}u+1$. The general form of a quadratic polynomial is $ax^2+bx+c, a\neq 0$ and a, b and c are real numbers.

A polynomial of degree 3 is called a **cubic polynomial**. Examples of cubic polynomials are $3-x^3, 3x^3+2+1, 5-u^2+5u^3$. The general form of a cubic polynomial is ax^3+bx^2+cx+d and a, b, c, d are real numbers.

Zero of a Polynomial

A real number k is said to be a zero of a polynomial $p(x)$, if $p(k)=0$. In general, if k is a zero of $p(x)=ax+b$, then $p(k)=ak+b=0$, i.e., $k=-\frac{b}{a}$. So, the zero of the linear polynomial $p(x)=ax+b$ is $-\frac{b}{a}=\frac{-(constant\ \ term)}{Coefficient\ \ of\ \ x}$. Thus, the zero of a linear polynomial is related to its coefficients.

Geometrical Meaning of the Zeroes of a Polynomial

Consider a linear polynomial $ax+b, a\neq 0$. We know that the graph of a linear polynomial is a straight line. For a linear polynomial $ax+b, a\neq 0$, the graph is a straight line which intersects the x-axis at exactly one point, namely, $\left(\frac{-b}{a},0\right)$. The zero of the linear polynomial is the x-coordinate of the point where the graph intersects the x-axis.

For any quadratic polynomial $ax^2+bx+c, a \neq 0$, the graph of the corresponding equation $y = ax^2+bx+c$ is a parabola and has one of the two shapes either open upwards like $\cup$ for $a > 0$ or open downwards like $\cap$ for $a > 0$.

The zeroes of a quadratic polynomial $ax^2+bx+c, a \neq 0$ are the x-coordinates of the points where the parabola representing $y = ax^2+bx+c$ intersects the x-axis.

The following three cases can happen:

1. The graph cuts the x-axis at two distinct points A and A'. The x-coordinates of A and A' are the two zeroes of the quadratic polynomial $ax^2+bx+c, a \neq 0$ in this case.
2. The graph cuts the x-axis at exactly one point. The x-coordinate of A is the only zero for the quadratic polynomial ax^2+bx+c.
3. The graph is either completely above the x-axis or completely below the x-axis. So, it does not cut the x-axis at any point. So, the quadratic polynomial ax^2+bx+c has no zero. Geometrically, therefore, a quadratic polynomial can have either two distinct zeroes or two equal zeroes or no zero. This means that a polynomial of degree 2 has atmost two zeroes.

Zeroes of a cubic polynomial

A cubic polynomial $ax^3+bx^2+cx+d, a \neq 0$ has at most 3 zeroes.

In general, **a polynomial *p(x)* of degree *n* has at most *n* zeroes. The graph of the polynomial *p(x)* intersects the *x*-axis at atmost *n* points.**

Let us find the number of zeroes in each of the following cases from the graphs of $y = p(x)$:

(i) Number of zeroes:No zero since the graph does not intersect the x-axis at any point.

(ii) Number of zeroes: 1 zero, since the graph intersects the x-axis at 1 point.

(iii) Number of zeroes: 3 zeroes, since the graph intersects the x-axis at 3 points.

(*iv*) Number of zeroes: 2 zeroes, since the graph intersects the x-axis at two points.

(*v*) Number of zeroes: 4 zeroes, since the graph intersects the x-axis at four points.

(*vi*) Number of zeroes: 3 zeroes, since the graph intersects the x-axis at three points.

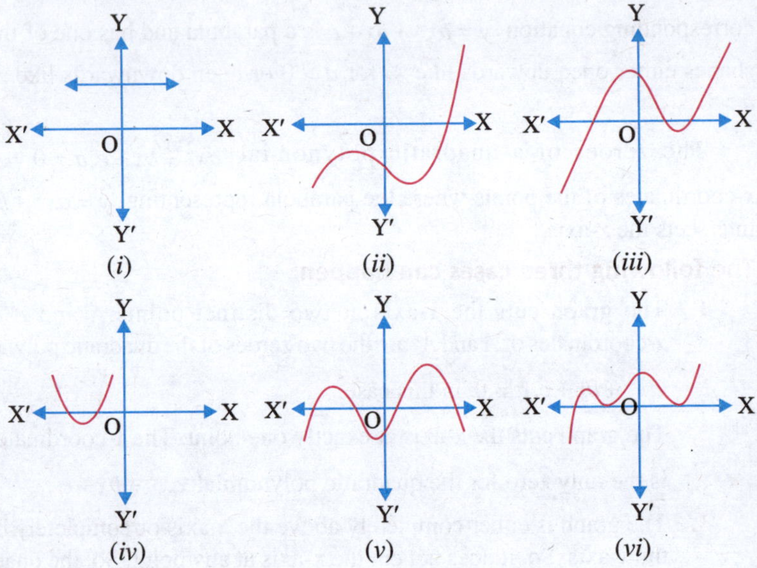

If α and β are the zeroes of the quadratic polynomial $ax^2+bx+c, a \neq 0$, then $x-\alpha$ and $x-\beta$ are the factors of $p(x)$. We can write

$$ax^2+bx+c = k(x-\alpha)(x-\beta), \text{ where } k \text{ is a constant}$$

$$= k\left[x^2-(\alpha+\beta)x+\alpha\beta\right]$$

$$= kx^2-k(\alpha+\beta)x+k\alpha\beta$$

Comparing the coefficients of x^2, x and constant terms on both sides, we get $a=k, b=-k(\alpha+\beta)$ and $c=k\alpha\beta$. This gives $\alpha+\beta=-\frac{b}{a}, \alpha\beta=\frac{c}{a}$.

To find a quadratic polynomial given the sum and product of zeroes: Let the quadratic polynomial be ax^2+bx+c, and its zeroes be α and β. We have, $\alpha+\beta=-\frac{b}{a}, \alpha\beta=\frac{c}{a}$. If $a=k$, then $b=-k$ (sum of zeroes) and $c=k$ (product of zeroes).

Type of Polynomial	General Form	No. of Zeroes	Relationship between Zeros
Linear	$ax+b, a \neq 0$	1	$k = -\frac{b}{a}$, *i.e.*, $k = -\frac{(\text{Constant term})}{(\text{Coefficient of } x)}$
Quadratic	$ax^2+bx+c, a \neq 0$	2	Sum of zeros $(\alpha+\beta) = -\frac{\text{Coefficient of } x}{\text{Coefficient of } x^2} = -\frac{b}{a}$ Product of zeros $(\alpha\,\beta) = \frac{\text{Constant term}}{\text{Coefficient of } x^2} = \frac{c}{a}$
Cubic	$ax^3+bx^2+cx+d, a \neq 0$	3	Sum of zeros $(\alpha+\beta+\gamma)$ $= -\frac{\text{Coefficient of } x^2}{\text{Coefficient of } x^3} = -\frac{b}{a}$ Sum of zeroes $(\alpha\beta\gamma)$ $= -\frac{\text{Constant term}}{\text{Coefficient of } x^3} = -\frac{d}{a}$ Product of zeros taken any at time $(\alpha\beta+\beta\gamma+\gamma\alpha)$ $= \frac{\text{Coefficient of } x}{\text{Coefficient of } x^3} = \frac{c}{a}$

Note :- Formation of a cubic polynomial : Let α, β and **γ** be the zeros of the polynomial. ∴ Required cubic polynomial $= (x-\alpha)(x-\beta)(x-\gamma)$.

Example: Let sum of zeroes = $\frac{1}{4}$, product of zeroes = –1.

Solution: We know that sum of zeroes $= -\frac{(\text{Coefficient of } x)}{\text{Coefficient of } x^2}$ and

$$\text{Product of zeroes} = \frac{\text{Constant term}}{\text{Coefficient of } x^2}.$$

Then, $\frac{1}{4} = -\frac{b}{a} \Rightarrow b = -\frac{a}{4}$ and $-1 = \frac{c}{a} \Rightarrow c = -a$ Let $a = k$ then $b = -\frac{k}{4}, c = -k$. We can write the quadratic polynomial as $p(x) = kx^2 - \frac{k}{4}x - k$, or,

$p(x) = k\left(x^2 - \frac{1}{4}x - 1\right)$. By taking different values of k, we can obtain different polynomials. By taking $k = 4$, we obtain, $p(x) = 4x^2 - x - 4$.

Division Algorithm for polynomials

If $p(x)$ and $g(x)$ are any two polynomials with $g(x) \neq 0$, then we can find polynomials $q(x)$and $r(x)$, such that $p(x) = g(x) \times q(x) + r(x)$, where $r(x) = 0$ or degree of $r(x)$ < degree of $g(x)$.

POINTS TO REMEMBER

1. The graph of a quadratic polynomial is a parabola.
2. The parabola opens upwards if the coefficient of x^2 is positive.
3. The parabola opens downwards if the coefficient of x^2 is negative
4. For the parabola $ax^2 + bx + c$, we have
   - *(i)* Vertex = $\left(-\frac{b}{2a}, -\frac{D}{4a}\right)$ where $D = b^2 - 4ac$
   - *(ii)* Axis of symmetry, $x = -\frac{b}{2a}$ parallel to y-axis
   - *(iii)* Zeroes are : $\frac{-b+\sqrt{b^2-4ac}}{2a}, \frac{-b-\sqrt{b^2-4ac}}{2a}$
   - *(iv)* If $D < 0$, a quad. Polynomial $ax^2 + bx + c$ has no real zeroes.
   - *(v)* If $D = 0$, a quad. Polynomial $ax^2 + bx + c$ has same real zeroes.
   - *(vi)* A quadratic polynomial has at most two real distinct zeroes only where $D \geq 0$.

(*vii*) Let α and β be the two real zeroes of the polynomial $ax^2 + bx + c$.

Therefore, $\alpha+\beta=-\frac{b}{a}$ and $\alpha\beta=\frac{c}{a}$

5. Division Algorithm : $p(x) = g(x) \cdot q(x) + r(x)$

$\Leftrightarrow$ $p(x) - r(x) = g(x) \cdot q(x)$

$p(x) - r(x)$ is a polynomial

degree $(p(x)) \geq$ degree $(g(x)) >$ degree $(r(x))$

$\Rightarrow$ degree $p(x) >$ degree $(r(x))$

$\Rightarrow$ degree $(p(x) - r(x)) = n$

[$\because$ The highest power term is not cancelled]

6. The zeroes of a polynomial $p(x)$ are x co-ordinates of the points where the graph of $y = p(x)$ intersects the x-axis.
7. A polynomial of degree n can have at most n zeroes.
8. If α, β, γ are the zeroes of the cubic polynomial ax^3+bx^2+cx+d ,

(*i*) $\alpha+\beta+\gamma=-\frac{b}{a}$

(*ii*) $\alpha\beta+\beta\gamma+\gamma\alpha=\frac{c}{a}$

(*iii*) $\alpha\beta\gamma=-\frac{d}{a}$

(*iv*) $ax^3+bx^2+cx+d=(x-\alpha)(x-\beta)(x-\gamma)$

9. A polynomial with integral coefficients is called a polynomial over the integers.
10. If $(x - a)$ is a factor of polynomial $f(x)$ of degree $n > 0$, then a is zero of the polynomial.

CHAPTER 3

PAIR OF LINEAR EQUATIONS IN TWO VARIABLES

1. An equation that can be written in the form $ax + by = c$, where $a \neq 0$, $b \neq 0$ and a, b and c are real numbers is known as a **linear equation in two variables x and y.**
2. Two linear equations containing the same two variables form a system of simultaneous linear equations, *e.g.*, $a_1x + b_1y = c_1$ and $a_2x + b_2y = c_2$ form a system of **simultaneous linear equations.**
3. A system of simultaneous linear equations in two variables is said to be **consistent** if the same values of x and y satisfy both the equations.
4. When the system of equations has a unique solution of the form $x = \alpha$, $y = \alpha$, it is called **consistent**.
5. When the system has no common solution, it is said to be **inconsistent**.
6. When the equations have infinitely many solutions, it is called **system of dependent equations.**
7. There are two methods of solving a system of linear equations in two variables:

   (*a*) Graphical

   (*b*) Algebraic
8. **Graphical method for solving a system of linear equations in two variables:**

   Consider a linear equation $ax + by = c$, where a, b, c are real numbers and $a \neq 0$, $b \neq 0$. Any pair of values of x and y which satisfy the equation is called its solution. Every linear equation in two variables has an infinite number of solutions. Every solution of the equation is a point on the line representing it.

   Let us summarise the behaviour of lines representing a pair of linear equations in two variables and the existence of solutions as follows:

   (*a*) If the lines intersect in a single point, the pair of equations has a unique solution or is said to be consistent.

(*b*) If the lines are parallel, the equations have no solution and are said to be inconsistent.

(*c*) If the lines are coincident, the equations have infinitely many solutions and are said to be dependent or consistent pair of equations.

Let (a_1, b_1) and (a_2, b_2) be any two solutions of the equation $ax + by = c$. To obtain the values (a_1, b_1) and (a_2, b_2), take different values of y and obtain the corresponding values of x by substituting in $x = \frac{c - by}{a}$.

Plot these values on a graph paper and join the points. We get a straight line which is the graph of the equation $ax + by = c$.

Take three points for drawing a graph and represent them in the form of a table.

Consider the equation $3x + 2y = 11$. Then, $x = \frac{11 - 2y}{3}$.

For $y = 1$, $x = (11 - 2)/3 = 3$

For $y = 4$, $x = (11 - 8)/3 = 1$

For $y = 7$, $x = (11 - 14)/3 = -1$

These values are represented in the following table and then a graph can be drawn by joining these points:

X	3	1	– 1
Y	1	4	7

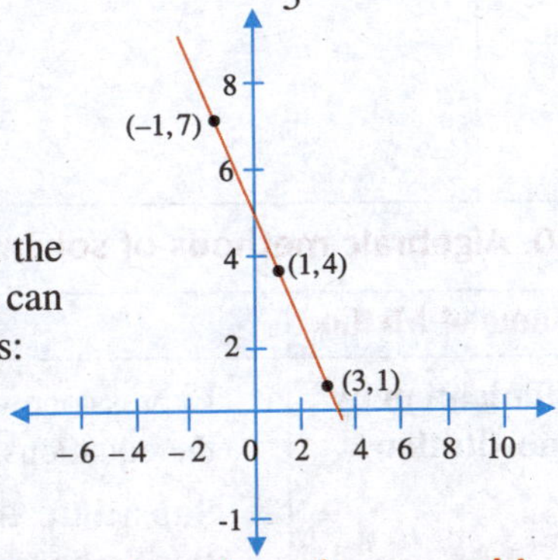

9. A summary of various types of questions based on graphical method is given below:

Type	Type of Problem	Method
I	**To draw a graph and to check whether a given ordered pair is a solution or not**	Represent the three ordered pairs which satisfy the given equation in a table. Plot these points on a graph paper. If the given point lies on the straight line, it is a solution.
II	**To solve a system of equations graphically and to check about consistency/ inconsistency of the system**	Plot the two sets of points on a single graph paper. We get two straight lines. If the two lines intersect, the system has a unique solution and is given by the point of intersection. If the two lines are parallel, the system has no solution. If the two lines are coincident, the system has infinite solutions.

III	**To plot a graph involving three equations and find vertices of the triangular region so formed. $X = 0$ is the Y-axis $Y = 0$ is the X-axis $X = a$ is a line parallel to the Y-axis at a distance of 'a' units from Y-axis. $Y = b$ is a line parallel to the X-axis at a distance of 'b' units from Y-axis.**	Find the points corresponding to the three equations. Represent them in a table.Find the points of intersection of the three lines taken two at a time from the graph. These points are the vertices of the triangle.
IV	**To find the area of triangle formed by three lines.**	Plot the points corresponding to the three lines on the same graph. If the triangle is formed with any one axis as the base, drop a perpendicular from the opposite vertex on the base.Read the length of the perpendicular from the graph.Area of triangle = ½ (Base × height)

10. Algebraic methods of solving the system of linear equations:

Name of Method	Steps
Elimination by Substitution	1. Express one variable in terms of the other in any one of the equations. 2. Substitute the value of the variable obtained in step-1 above in the 2nd equation. 3. Solve the equation obtained and find the value of the variable. 4. Substitute the value of this variable in any of the equations and find the value of the other variable.
Elimination by Equating the coefficients	1. Multiply the given equations by the LCM of the coefficients of any variable so as to make the coefficient of the variable equal in both the equations. 2. Subtract the equations obtained above if the coefficients have the same sign. 3. Add the two equations obtained in step-1 if the two equations have opposite signs. 4. Solve the equation obtained in above step as it is a linear equation in one variable. 5. Substitute the value of variable obtained in above in any of the equations and obtain the value of the other variable.

Method of Cross-multiplication	**1.** For the equations $a_1x + b_1y = c_1$ and $a_2x + b_2y = c_2$, $\frac{x}{b_1c_2 - b_2c_1} = \frac{y}{c_1a_2 - c_2a_1} = \frac{-1}{a_1b_2 - a_2b_1}$
Special Equations ***TYPE - 1:*** ***ax + by = cxy;*** ***dx + ey = fxy*** ***TYPE - II:*** $\frac{p}{ax+by} + \frac{q}{cx+dy} = e$ $\frac{r}{ax+by} + \frac{s}{cx+dy} = f$ ***TYPE - III:*** *ax + by = c;* *bx + ay = d*	*We have two types of solutions:* *1.* ***Trivial solution****: when x = 0, y = 0* *2.* ***Non-trivial solution*** *when $x \neq 0$ and $y \neq 0$. To find its solution, divide both equations by xy and then let 1/x = u and 1/y = v.* *Let* $\frac{1}{ax+by} = u$ *and* $\frac{1}{cx+dy} = v$ *Solve the equations obtained for u and v. Substitute the values of u and v and solve for x and y. Add both the equations and reduce it to the simpler form by dividing it by (a + b). Subtract the 1st equation from the 2nd and reduce it to a simpler form by (a – b).Solve the equations obtained above for x and y.*

Condition for Solvability

For a system of linear equations in two variables, $a_1x + b_1y = c_1$ and $a_2x + b_2y = c_2$, we can summarize the conditions for solvability as:

Unique Solution	$\frac{a_1}{a_2} \neq \frac{b_1}{b_2}$	**Find the value of k for which the system of equations, $x + 2y = 5$ and $3x + ky + 15 = 0$ has a unique solution.** For unique solution, $\frac{a_1}{a_2} \neq \frac{b_1}{b_2}$. Here a_1=1, b_1=2, a_2= 3, b_2= k. We have, $\frac{1}{3} \neq \frac{2}{k}$, or $k \neq 6$
No Solution	$\frac{a_1}{a_2} = \frac{b_1}{b_2} \neq \frac{c_1}{c_2}$	**Find the value of *k* for which the system of equations, $x + 2y = 3$ and $(k - 1)x + (k + 1)y = k + 2$ has no solutions.** Here a_1=1, b_1=2, c_1= 3 and $a_2 = (k-1)$, $b_2 = (k+1)$, $c_2 = k + 2$. Condition for no solution is $\frac{a_1}{a_2} = \frac{b_1}{b_2} \neq \frac{c_1}{c_2}$. Putting these values, we have, $\frac{1}{k-1} = \frac{2}{k+1} \neq \frac{3}{k+2}$. *i.e.,* $\frac{1}{k-1} = \frac{2}{k+1}$

		and $\frac{2}{k+1} \neq \frac{3}{k+2}$ .Solving these two equations, we get $k = 3$ or $k \neq 1$
Infinite Solutions	$\frac{a_1}{a_2} = \frac{b_1}{b_2} = \frac{c_1}{c_2}$	***Find the value of k for which the system of equations have infinite solutions: kx + 3y = 2k + 1, and 2 (k +1) x + 9y = 7k + 1*** Here, $a_1=k$, $b_1= 3$, $c_1=2k + 1$, $a_2=2 (k+1)$, $b_2=9$, $c_2= 7k + 1$. *For infinite solution,* $\frac{a_1}{a_2} = \frac{b_1}{b_2} = \frac{c_1}{c_2}$, *or,* $\frac{k}{2(k+1)} = \frac{3}{9} = \frac{2k+1}{7k+1}$. *Solving, we get* $9k = 6k + 6$, or $3k = 6$, or $k = 2$

Word Problems

Problem Type	Steps to be followed
1. Age problems	If the problem involves finding out the ages of two persons, take the present age of one person as x and of the other as y. Then, 'a' years ago, age of 1st person was '$x - a$' years and that of 2nd person was '$y - a$', and after 'b' years, age of 1st person will be '$x + b$' years and that of 2nd person will be '$y + b$' years.Formulate the equations and then solve them.
2. Problems based on Numbers and Digits	Let the digit at Unit's place be x and that at Ten's place be y. The two-digit number is given by $10\,y + x$. On interchanging the positions of the digits, the digit at Unit's place becomes y and at Ten's place becomes x. The two digit number becomes $10\,x + y$. Formulate the equations and then solve them.
3. Problems based on fractions	Let the numerator of the fraction be x and denominator be y. Then the fraction $= \frac{x}{y}$. Formulate the linear equations on the basis of conditions given and solve for x and y to get the value of the fraction.
4. Problems based on Distance, Speed and Time	We know that Speed is defined as, Speed $= \frac{\text{Distance}}{\text{Time}}$, Distance = Speed × Time and Time $= \frac{\text{Distance}}{\text{Speed}}$.

	To solve problems related to speed of boat going downstream and upstream, let the speed of boat in still water be x km/hr, and speed of stream be y km/h. then, the speed of boat in downstream = $(x + y)$ km/h and speed of boat in upstream = $(x - y)$ km/h.
5. Problems based on Commercial Mathematics	For solving specific questions based on Commercial Mathematics, the fare of 1 Full Ticket may be taken as Rs. x and the reservation charges may be taken as Rs. y, so that one full fare = $x + y$ and one half fare = $\frac{x}{2} + y$. To solve questions of profit and loss, take the cost price of 1st article as Rs. x and that of 2nd article as Rs. y. To solve questions based on Simple interest, take the amount invested as Rs. x at some rate of interest and Rs. y at some other rate of interest.
6. Problems based on Geometry and Mensuration	Make use of the angle sum property of a triangle ($\angle A + \angle B + \angle C = 180^\circ$) in case of a triangle. In case of a parallelogram, opposite angles are equal and in case of a cyclic quadrilateral, opposite angles are supplementary.

CHAPTER 4

QUADRATIC EQUATIONS

1. Quadratic polynomial

A polynomial of the type $p(x) = ax^2 + bx + c$, where $a \neq 0$ and a, b, c are real numbers is called a quadratic polynomial.

2. Quadratic Equation

An equation $p(x) = 0$ where $p(x)$ is a quadratic polynomial is called a quadratic equation and can be written as $ax^2 + bx + c = 0$, where $a \neq 0$.

3. Examples of Quadratic equations:

(i) $(x-2)^2 + 1 = x^2 - 4x + 5$

(ii) $x(2x+3) = 2x^2 + 3x$

4. Roots of Quadratic Equations

Those values of x which satisfy the quadratic equation $ax^2 + bx + c = 0$ are called zeroes of the quadratic equation. If α, β are zeroes of the polynomial $ax^2 + bx + c$, then α, β are called roots of the corresponding equation $ax^2 + bx + c = 0$. This implies that $p(\alpha) = p(\beta) = 0$. We can write it as $a\alpha^2 + b\alpha + c = 0$ and $a\beta^2 + b\beta + c = 0$. The zeroes of the quadratic polynomial $ax^2 + bx + c$ and the roots of the quadratic equation $ax^2 + bx + c = 0$ are same.

5. Solution of Quadratic Equation

The roots of a quadratic equation can be found by two methods:

(*i*) By Factorization method

The quadratic polynomial $ax^2 + bx + c$ can be expressed as the product of two linear factors, say $(px+q)$ and p, q, r, s, where p, q, r, s are real numbers and $p \neq 0, r \neq 0$. Then we can write the quadratic equation $ax^2 + bx + c = 0$ as, $(px + q)\ (rx + s) = 0$

or, $(px+q)=0$ or, $(rx+s)=0$.

Solving these linear equations, we get the roots as,

$$x=-\frac{q}{p} \text{ and } x=\frac{-s}{r}$$

(ii) By completion of square (Sridharacharya's Rule) Ist Method :

Consider the quadratic equation $ax^2+bx+c=0$. Let us complete the square so that we can express this quadratic equation as a perfect square.

Step-1: Dividing the quadratic equation by a, we get, $x^2+\frac{b}{a}x+\frac{c}{a}=0$.

Step-2: Transposing, we get, $x^2+\frac{b}{a}x=-\frac{c}{a}$.

Step-3: Adding $\left(\frac{1}{2}coeff.\ of\ x\right)^2$, *i.e*, $\left(\frac{b}{2a}\right)^2$ to both sides, we get

$$x^2+\frac{b}{a}x+\left(\frac{b}{2a}\right)^2=-\frac{c}{a}+\left(\frac{b}{2a}\right)^2 \text{ or } \left(x+\frac{b}{2a}\right)^2=\frac{b^2}{4a^2}-\frac{c}{a}=\frac{b^2-4ac}{4a^2}$$

Step-4: Taking square root to both sides, we get

$$x+\frac{b}{2a}=\pm\frac{\sqrt{b^2-4ac}}{2a}$$

Step-5: Solving for x, we get, $x=-\frac{b}{2a}\pm\frac{\sqrt{b^2-4ac}}{2a}=\frac{-b\pm\sqrt{b^2-4ac}}{2a}$

So, the roots of the quadratic equation $ax^2+bx+c=0$ are

$$x=\frac{-b+\sqrt{b^2-4ac}}{2a}, \text{ or, } x=\frac{-b-\sqrt{b^2-4ac}}{2a}$$

IInd Method

$$ax^2+bx+c=0 \quad\Rightarrow\quad ax^2+bx=-c$$

Multiply both sides by $4a$

$$4a^2x^2+4abx=-4ac$$

Add both sides b^2, we get

$$4a^2x^2+4abx+b^2=b^2-4ac \quad\Rightarrow\quad (2ax)^2+2.2ax.b+b^2=b^2-4ac$$

$$\Rightarrow\quad (2ax+b)^2=b^2-4ac \quad\Rightarrow\quad 2ax+b=\pm\sqrt{b^2-4ac}$$

$$\Rightarrow\quad 2ax=-b\pm\sqrt{b^2-4ac} \quad\Rightarrow\quad x=\frac{-b\pm\sqrt{b^2-4ac}}{2a}$$

$$\alpha=\frac{-b+\sqrt{b^2-4ac}}{2a} \text{ and } \beta=\frac{-b-\sqrt{b^2-4ac}}{2a}$$

Nature of Roots

The nature of roots of a given quadratic equation can be found by determining the value of $b^2 - 4ac$ known as the **Discriminant**.

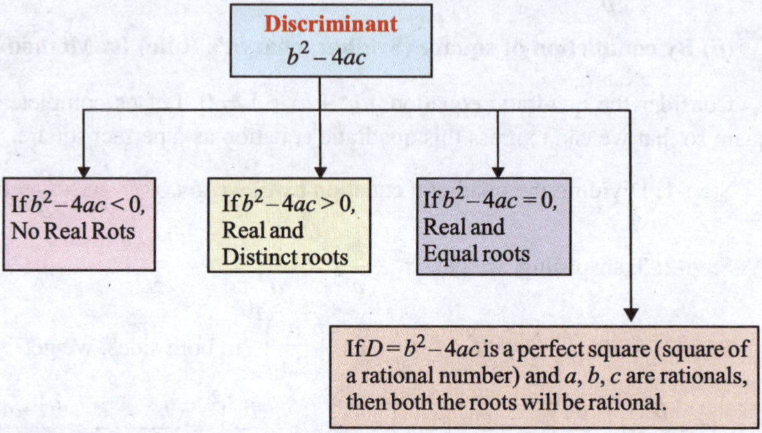

Therefore, for a given quadratic equation, the condition for real roots is: $D \geq 0$, or, $b^2 - 4ac \geq 0$.

We should also remember the following results as they will be useful in finding the nature of roots.

I. $x^2 - a^2 \geq 0 \quad \Rightarrow \quad x \leq -a$ or $x \geq a$

II. $x^2 - a^2 < 0 \quad \Rightarrow \quad -a < x < a$

Relation Between root of quadratic equations and Coefficients

1. If α and β are the roots of the equation $ax^2 + bx + c = 0$, then

(*a*) $(x - \alpha)(x - \beta) = ax^2 + bx + c$.

(*b*) Sum of the roots, $\alpha + \beta = \frac{-b}{a} = -\frac{\text{Coefficient of } x}{\text{Coefficient of } x^2}$

(*c*) Product of the roots, $\alpha\beta = \frac{c}{a} = \frac{\text{Constant term}}{\text{Coefficient of } x^2}$

2. Formation of Quadratic equation

The quadratic equation whose roots are α and β is $x^2 - (\alpha + \beta)x + \alpha\beta = 0$.

or x^2 – (Sum of the roots) x + (Product of roots) = 0

USEFUL RESULTS

- $\alpha^2+\beta^2=(\alpha+\beta)^2-2\alpha\beta$
- $\alpha^3+\beta^3=(\alpha+\beta)^3-3\alpha\beta(\alpha+\beta)$
- $(\alpha-\beta)^2=(\alpha+\beta)^2-4\alpha\beta$
- $\alpha^2-\beta^2=(\alpha+\beta)(\alpha-\beta)=\pm(\alpha+\beta)\sqrt{(\alpha+\beta)^2-4\alpha\beta}$
- $\alpha^3-\beta^3=(\alpha-\beta)(\alpha^2+\alpha\beta+\beta^2)=\pm[(\alpha+\beta)^2-\alpha\beta]\sqrt{(\alpha+\beta)^2-4\alpha\beta}$
- $\alpha^4+\beta^4=(\alpha^2+\beta^2)^2-2\alpha^2\beta^2=[(\alpha+\beta)^2-2\alpha\beta]^2-2(\alpha\beta)^2$
- $\alpha^4-\beta^4=(\alpha^2+\beta^2)(\alpha+\beta)(\alpha-\beta)$

  $=\pm[(\alpha+\beta)^2-2\alpha\beta](\alpha+\beta)\sqrt{(\alpha+\beta)^2-4\alpha\beta}$.

CHAPTER 5

ARITHMETIC PROGRESSIONS

Sequence

A succession of numbers formed and arranged according to some definite law is called a sequence. For example 3, 7, 11, 15,..... or 2, 4, 16,......

Progression

If the terms of a series constantly increase or decrease in numerical value, the series is called a progression.

Arithmetic Progression

Arithmetic progression is a set of numbers in which each successive number can be formed by adding a fixed number to the previous number. The fixed number is known as the common difference, denoted by **'*d*'**. It can be positive, negative or zero. The first term is denoted by **'*a*'**. The successive terms of the sequence (A.P.) are given by

$$a, a+d, a+2d, a+3d, ...$$

There are two types of A.P.

Finite AP and Infinite AP. There are only a finite number of terms in a finite AP and it has a last term. If the number of terms in an AP is not finite and does not have a last term, it is known as an infinite AP.

The *n*th term of an AP whose first term is **'*a*'** and common difference is **'*d*'** is given by

$$\boxed{T_n = a_n = a + (n-1)d}$$

. It is sometimes denoted as '*l*' also.

The sum of first n terms of an AP having its first term as **'*a*'** and common difference as **'*d*'** is given by

$$\boxed{S_n = \frac{n}{2}[2a + (n-1)d]}$$

If we denote the last term of the AP, a_n by l, we can write the sum formula as $S_n = \frac{n}{2}(a + l)$.

Sum of first *n*-Natural Number

$$1+2+3+4+5+\ldots+n = S_n = \sum_{k=1}^{n} k = \frac{n(n+1)}{2}$$

Sum of the Squares of first *n*-Natural Numbers

$$S_n = 1^2+2^2+3^2+\ldots+n^2 = \sum_{k=1}^{n} k^2 = \frac{n(n+1)(2n+1)}{6}$$

Sum of the Cubes of first *n* Natural Number

$$S_n = 1^3+2^3+3^3+\ldots+n^3 = \sum_{k=1}^{n} k^3 = \left[\frac{n(n+1)}{2}\right]^2$$

The nth term of an AP is the difference of the sum to first *n* terms and the sum to first $(n-1)$ terms of it, *i.e.*, $a_n = S_n - S_{n-1}$.

There may be two values of *n* for which the sum of an AP is zero. This is because when a is positive and *d* is negative, some terms will be positive and some others negative, and will cancel out each other.

nth Term from the end of an AP

In an AP with first term = *a*, common difference = *d* and the last term = *l*, then the *n*th **Term from the end** = $[l-(n-1)d]$.

Arithmetic Mean (AM)

If *a*, *A*, *b* are in *AP*, we say that *A* is the arithmetic mean (abbreviated as AM) between *a* and *b*.

The AM between *a* and $b = \frac{1}{2}(a+b)$

Finding Terms of an AP

It is always convenient to make a choice of

(*i*) 3 numbers in AP as $(a-d), a, (a+d)$

(*ii*) 4 numbers in AP as $(a-3d), (a-d), (a+d), (a+3d)$

(*iii*) 5 numbers in AP as $(a-2d), (a-d), a, (a+d), (a+2d)$

(*iv*) 6 numbers in AP as $(a-5d), (a-3d), (a-d), (a+d), (a+3d), (a+5d)$.

Some Useful Properties of A.P.

If $a_1, a_2, a_3, \ldots, a_n$ are in A.P. then

- $a_1+k, a_2+k, \ldots, a_n+k$ are also in A.P.
- $a_1-k, a_2-k, \ldots, a_n-k$ are also in A.P.
- $ka_1, ka_2, \ldots, ka_n$ are also in A.P.
- $\frac{a_1}{k}, \frac{a_2}{k}, \ldots, \frac{a_n}{k}, k \neq 0$ are also in A.P.

CHAPTER 6

TRIANGLES

1. Similar Figures :

Geometric figures having the same shape but different sizes are known as similar figures.

Two congruent figures are always similar but two similar figures need not be congruent.

Examples: (*a*) Any two rectangles are similar

(*b*) Any two squares are similar.

(*c*) Any two circles are similar.

2. Similar Polygons :

Two polygons are said to be similar, if

(*a*) Their corresponding angles are equal, and

(*b*) The lengths of their corresponding sides are proportional.

If two polygons $ABCDE$ and $PQRST$ are similar, we write $ABCDE \sim PQRST$, where the symbol '~' stands for 'is similar to'

Triangles

A plane figure bounded by three line segments is called a triangle.

We denote a triangle by the symbol Δ.

Types of Triangles

1. **Scalene triangle**

   A triangle is called a scalene triangle if lengths of its sides are not equal to one another.

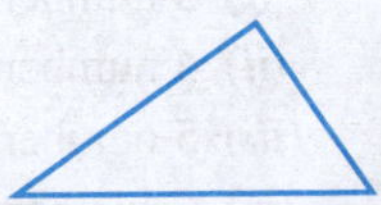

2. **Isosceles Triangles**

   A triangles is called an isosceles triangles if lengths of any two *of the three* sides of the triangle are equal.

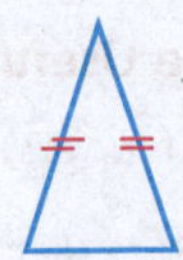

3. **Equilateral Triangles**

   A triangles is called an equilateral triangle if lengths of all the three sides of the triangle are equal. Each angle of an equilateral triangle 60°.

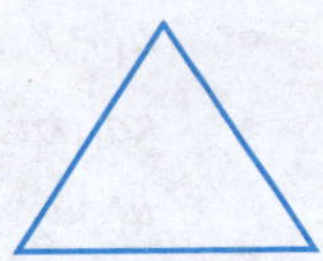

4. Acute Angled Triangle

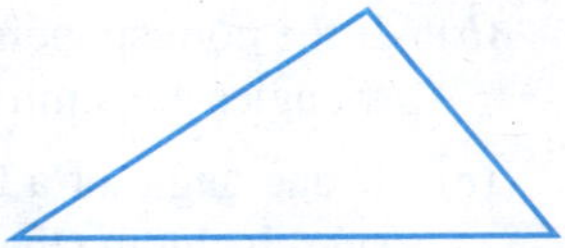

A triangle is called acute angled triangle if all the three angles are acute angles (< 90°).

5. Obtuse Angled Triangle

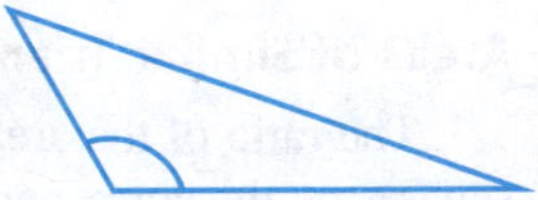

A triangle is called an obtuse angled triangle if one of its angle is an obtuse angle (> 90°).

6. Right Angled Triangle

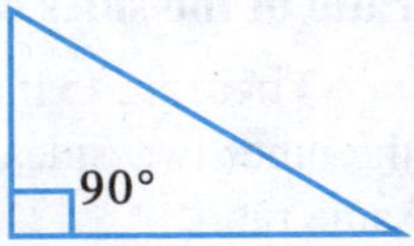

A triangle is called a right angled triangle if one of its angle is a right angle (90°). The side opposite to the right angle in a right-angled triangle is called its **'Hypotenuse'**. If lengths of the two sides containing the right angle in a right angled triangle are equal, then it is called a right angled isosceles triangle.

7. Similar Triangles:

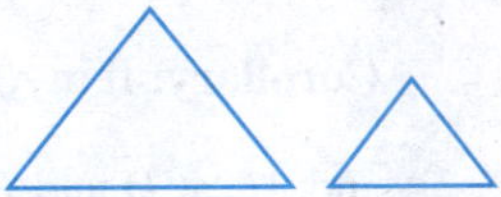

Two triangles are said to be similar if

(a) their corresponding angles are equal and

(b) their corresponding sides are proportional.

Trisection

The point which divideds *AB* in the ratio of 1 : 2 or 2 : 1 is called point of trisection.

Basic Proportionality Theorem (Thale's Theorem):

In a triangle, a line drawn parallel to one side, to intersect the other two sides in distinct points, divides the two sides in the same ratio.

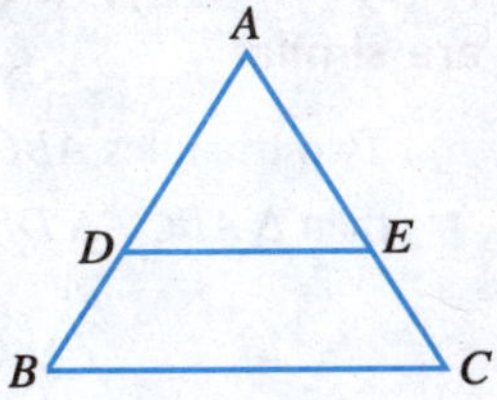

Since DE || BC

$$\frac{AD}{BD} = \frac{AE}{CE} \quad \text{or} \quad \frac{AB}{AC} = \frac{BD}{CE} = \frac{AD}{AE}$$

Converse of Basic Proportionality Theorem:

If a line divides any two sides of a triangle in the same ratio, the line must be parallel to the third side.

Similarity of Triangles:

(a) If in two triangles, the corresponding angles are equal, then the triangles are similar. [*AAA Similarity*]

(*b*) If the corresponding sides of two triangles are proportional then the triangles are similar. [*SSS Similarity*]

(*c*) If one angle of a triangle is equal to one angle of the other and the sides including these angles are proportional, the triangles are similar. [*SAS Similarity*]

Areas of Similar Triangles

The ratio of the areas of two similar triangles is equal to the ratio of the squares on the corresponding sides.

The bisector of an angle of a triangle divides the opposite side in the ratio of the sides containing the angle.

Theorem 1: If a line is drawn parallel to one side of a triangle, to intersect the other two sides in distinct points, the other two sides are divided in the same ratio.

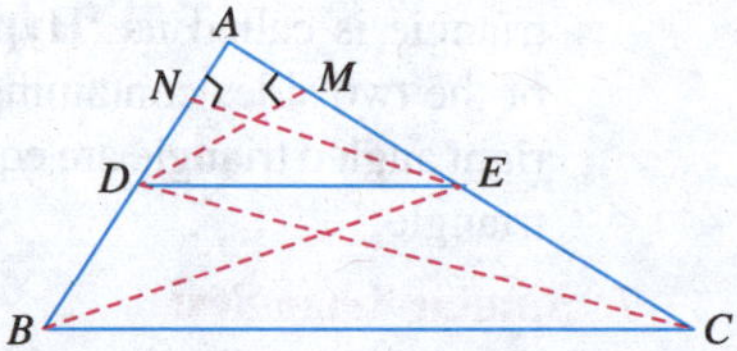

That is, given a ΔABC in which a line parallel to BC intersects the side AB at D and side AC at E. Then, $\dfrac{AD}{DB} = \dfrac{AE}{EC}$

Corollary: If in ΔABC, a line parallel to BC intersects other two sides AB and AC at D and E respectively, then $\dfrac{AD}{DB} = \dfrac{AE}{EC}$. ... (*i*)

Adding 1 to both sides, we get $\dfrac{AB}{DB} = \dfrac{AC}{EC}$.

Taking reciprocal, we get $\dfrac{DB}{AB} = \dfrac{EC}{AC}$. ... (*ii*)

Multiplying, (*i*) and (*ii*) we get $\dfrac{AD}{DB} \times \dfrac{DB}{AB} = \dfrac{AE}{EC} \times \dfrac{EC}{AC} \Rightarrow \dfrac{AD}{AB} = \dfrac{AE}{AC}$

(AAA Similarity) If two triangles are equiangular, then the triangles are similar

Two triangles ABC and DEF such that $\angle A = \angle D, \angle B = \angle E, \ \angle C = \angle F$, then $\Delta ABC \sim \Delta DEF$.

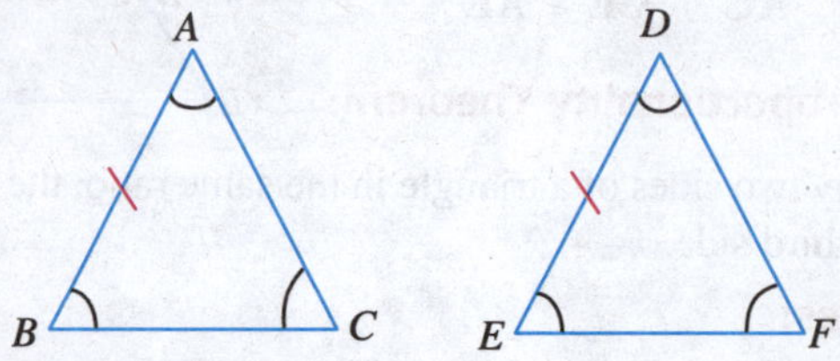

The corresponding sides are proportional, *i.e.*, $\dfrac{AB}{DE} = \dfrac{BC}{EF} = \dfrac{AC}{DF}$.

AA corollary

If two angles of one triangle are respectively equal to two angles of another triangle, then the two triangles are similar.

SSS Similarity

If the corresponding sides of two triangles are proportional the two triangles are similar.

SAS Similarity

If in two triangles, one pair of corresponding sides is proportional and the included angles are equal, the two triangles are similar.

The ratio of the areas of two similar triangles is equal to the ratio of the squares of their corresponding sides. Given ΔABC and ΔPQR such that $\Delta ABC \sim PQR$.

Then, $$\frac{\text{area } (\Delta ABC)}{\text{area } (\Delta PQR)} = \frac{AB^2}{PQ^2} = \frac{BC^2}{QR^2} = \frac{CA^2}{RP^2}$$

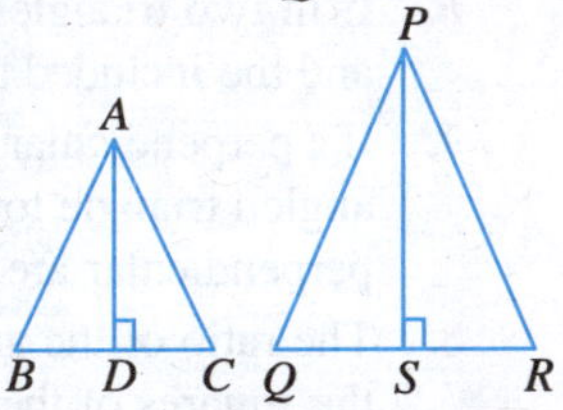

Pythagoras Theorem

In a right-angled triangle, the square on the hypotenuse is equal to the sum of the squares on the other two sides.

$$h^2 = p^2 + b^2$$

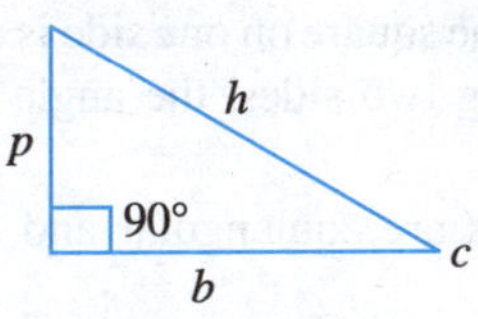

Given a right angled triangle ABC, right angled at B. Then,

$$AC^2 = AB^2 + BC^2$$

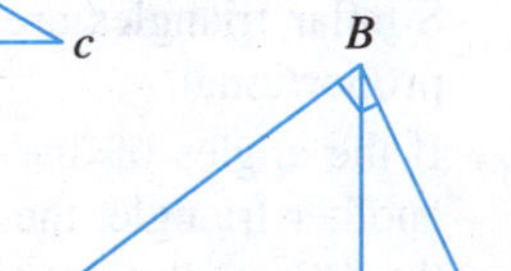

Converse of Pythagoras theorem

In a triangle, if the square of one side is equal to the sum of the squares of the other two sides, then the angle opposite to the first side is a right angle.

Similarity of triangles formed by an altitude of a right triangle

If a perpendicular is drawn from the vertex of the right angle of a right triangle to the hypotenuse, the triangles on each side of the perpendicular are similar to the whole triangle and to each other. In the triangle ABC right angled at B, the two triangles ABD and BCD are similar because $\angle A$ *of* $\Delta ABD = \angle CBD$ *of* ΔCBD and $\angle ADB$ *of* $\Delta ABD = \angle CDB$ of ΔCBD.

POINTS TO REMEMBER

1. If a line is drawn parallel to one side of a triangle, the other two sides are divided in the same ratio.
2. If a line divides any two sides of a triangle in the same ratio, the line must be parallel to the third side.
3. If in two triangles, the corresponding angles are equal (*i.e.*, the two triangles are equiangular), their corresponding sides are proportional.
4. If the corresponding sides of two triangles are proportional then the triangles are similar.
5. If the corresponding sides of two triangles are proportional, the triangles are equiangular.
6. If in two triangles, one pair of corresponding sides are proportional and the included angles are equal then the two triangles are similar.
7. If a perpendicular is drawn from the vertex of the right angle of a right angled triangle to the hypotenuse, the triangles on each side of the perpendicular are similar to the whole triangle and to each other.
8. The ratio of the areas of two similar triangles is equal to the ratio of the squares of their corresponding sides.
9. In a right triangle, the square on the hypotenuse is equal to the sum of the squares of the other two sides.
10. In a triangle, if the square on one side is equal to the sum of the squares on the remaining two sides, the angle opposite to the first side is a right angle.
11. Similar triangles are equiangular and their corresponding sides are proportional.
12. If the angles of one triangle are respectively equal to the angles of another triangle, the ratio of the corresponding sides is the same as the ratio of the corresponding:
    (*i*) medians (*ii*) bisectors of angles (*iii*) altitude.
13. The perimeters of two similar triangles are proportional to the ratio of their corresponding sides.
14. Sum of the squares of the sides of a Rhombus is equal to the sum of the squares of its diagonals.
15. The sum of squares of the diagonals of a parallelogram is equal to the sum of the squares of its sides.
16. If any triangle the sum of the squares on any two sides is equal to twice the square on half of third side together with twice the square on the median which bisects the third side.

    Or

    If AD is the median of a triangle ABC, then $AB^2 + AC^2 = 2BD^2 + 2AD^2$
    This Result is known as **Apollonius Theorem**.

CHAPTER 7

CO-ORDINATE GEOMETRY

STRAIGHT LINE

Rectangular Axis

Let $X' OX$, $Y' OY$ be two straight lines whose positive direction is shown by the arrow and which meet at right angles at O (origin).

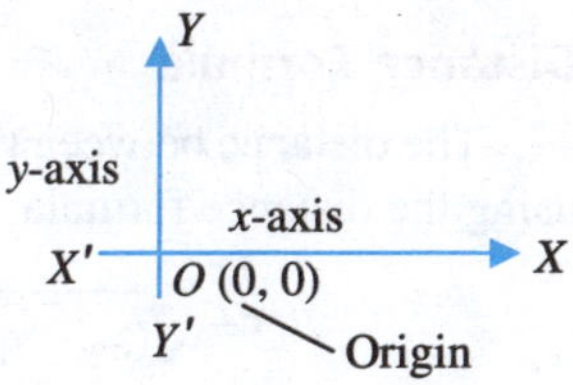

Then

(*a*) $X' OX$ is called axis of x or the x-axis.

(*b*) $Y' OY$ is called axis of y or the y-axis.

Co-ordinates

Let P be a point in the plane of the rectangular axis. From P draw PM perpendicular on the x-axis. Then

(*i*) Length OM is called abscissa of P and is denoted by x.

(*ii*) Length MP is called ordinate of P and is denoted by y.

(*iii*) The two together taken in this order are called co-ordinates of P and are denoted by (x, y).

Where, x is x co-ordinate and y is y co-ordinate

(*iv*) Point of intersection of the co-ordinate axis is called origin.

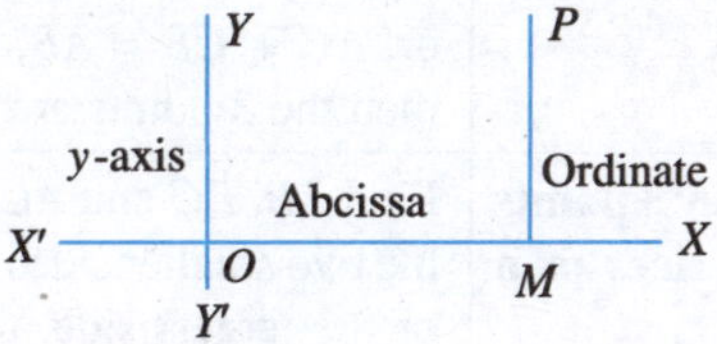

Rule for Signs of Co-ordinates

1. x or abscissa is +ve if it is measured to the right of the origin and –ve if measure to the left of the origin.

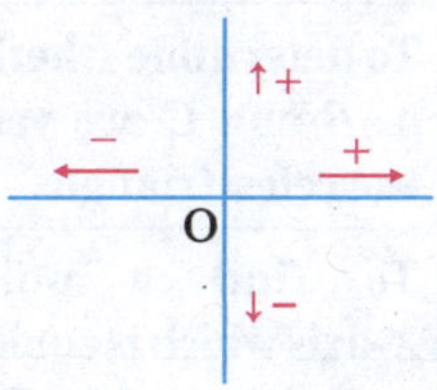

2. y or ordinate is +ve if it is measured above the x-axis and –ve if measured below the x-axis.

Quadrants

The two axes divide the plane into four parts called quadrants. The signs of the coordinates of points in different quadrants are given below:

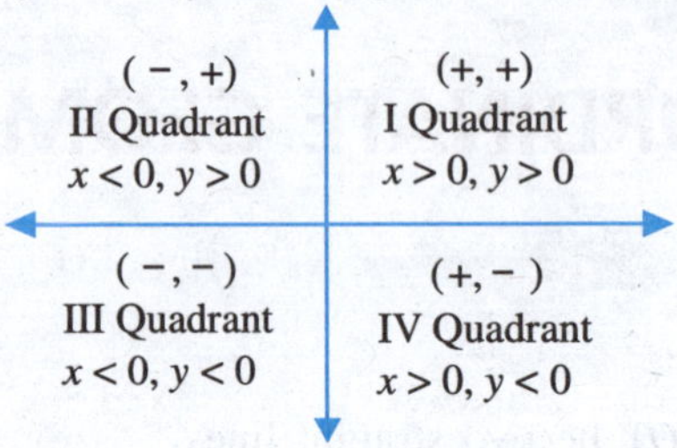

Distance Formula

The distance between two points $P(x_1, y_1)$ and $Q(x_2, y_2)$ can be found by using the distance formula,

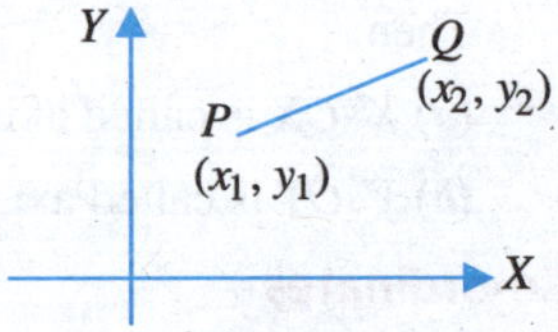

$$PQ = \sqrt{(x_2 - x_1)^2 + (y_2 - y_1)^2}$$

Or

$$\sqrt{(x_1 - x_2)^2 + (y_1 - y_2)^2}$$

Remarks: The distance of a point $P(x, y)$ from the origin $O(0, 0)$ is given by $OP = \sqrt{x^2 + y^2}$.

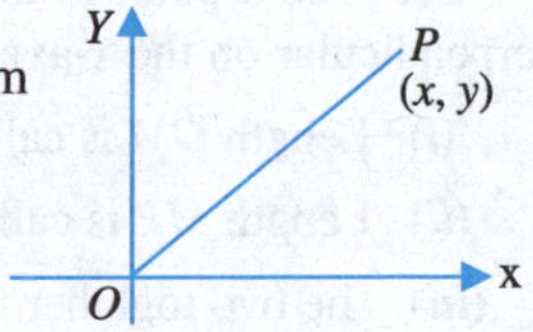

Applications of Distance Formula:

Type of problem	Solution
To determine whether 3 given points *A*, *B* and *C* are collinear.	Find *AB*, *BC* and *AC*. If sum of any two is equal to the third, *i.e.*, if $AB + BC = AC$, or, $AC + CB = AB$, or $CA + AB = CB$, then the 3 points are collinear.
To determine whether 3 points *A*, *B* and *C* are vertices of a right triangle.	Find *AB*, *BC* and *AC*. If sum of square of the two smaller sides is equal to the square of the largest side, the three points form vertices of a right triangle.
To determine whether 3 points *A*, *B* and *C* are vertices of an isosceles triangle.	Find *AB*, *BC* and *AC*. If any two sides are equal, the three points form vertices of an isosceles triangle.
To find a point *A* on X-axis which is equidistant from two given points $P(x_1, y_1)$ and $Q(x_2, y_2)$.	The coordinates of the point *A* on the X-axis will be $(x, 0)$. Then using $PA = PB$, or $PA^2 = PB^2$, x can be found.

To find a point A on Y-axis which is equidistant from two given points $P(x_1, y_1)$ and $Q(x_2, y_2)$.	The coordinates of the point A on the Y-axis will be $(0, y)$.Then using $PA = PB$, or $PA^2 = PB^2$, y can be found.
To determine whether 4 given points A, B, C and D form vertices of a rhombus.	Find AB, BC, CD and DA.Also find the lengths of their diagonals AC and BD.If $AB = BC = CD = DA$ and Diagonal $AC \neq$ Diagonal BD, the 4 points form vertices of a rhombus.
To determine whether 4 given points A, B, C and D form vertices of a square.	Find AB, BC, CD and DA.Also find the lengths of their diagonals AC and BD.If $AB = BC = CD = DA$ and Diagonal $AC =$ Diagonal BD, the 4 points form vertices of a square.
To determine whether 4 given points A, B, C and D form vertices of a parallelogram.	Find AB, BC, CD and DA.If $AD = BC$ and $AB = CD$ the 4 points form vertices of a parallelogram.
To determine whether 4 given points A, B, C and D form vertices of a rectangle.	Find AB, BC, CD and DA.If $AD = BC$ and $AB = CD$ and the Diagonal $AC =$ Diagonal BD, the 4 points form vertices of a rectangle.

Section Formula

The coordinates of a point A, which divide the linesegment joining two points $P(x_1, y_1)$ and $Q(x_2, y_2)$ internally in the ratio m : n are given by

$$x = \frac{mx_2 + nx_1}{m+n} \text{ and } y = \frac{my_2 + ny_1}{m+n}.$$

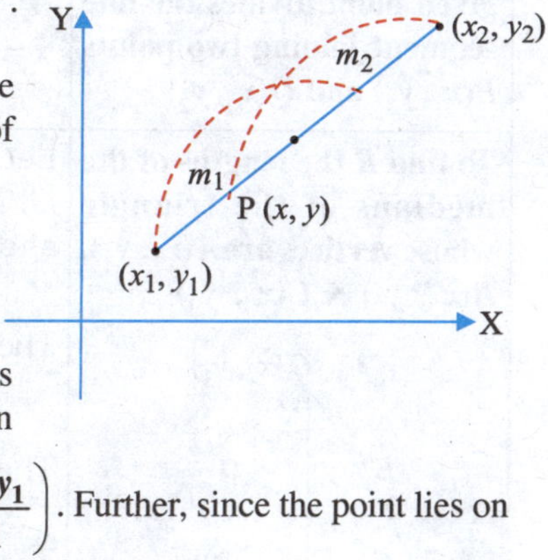

If the ratio in which P divides the line segment AB is $k : 1$, then the coordinates of the point P will be

$$\left(\frac{kx_2 + x_1}{k+1}, \frac{ky_2 + y_1}{k+1}\right).$$

To find the ratio in which the x-axis divides the line segment joining two given points, use the formula $\left(\frac{kx_2 + x_1}{k+1}, \frac{ky_2 + y_1}{k+1}\right)$. Further, since the point lies on the x-axis, and we know that on the x-axis the ordinate y is 0. Therefore,

$$\left(\frac{ky_2 + y_1}{k+1}\right) = 0.$$

To find the ratio in which the y-axis divides the line segment joining two given points, use the formula $\left(\dfrac{kx_2 + x_1}{k+1}, \dfrac{ky_2 + y_1}{k+1}\right)$. Further, since the point lies on the y-axis, and we know that on the y-axis the abscissa x is 0. Therefore, $\left(\dfrac{kx_2 + x_1}{k+1}\right) = 0$.

Mid-point formula

The coordinates of the mid-point of the line-segment joining the two points $P(x_1, y_1)$ and $Q(x_2, y_2)$ are given by

$$\left\{x = \frac{x_1 + x_2}{2}, y = \frac{y_1 + y_2}{2}\right\}$$

Coordinates of Centroid

The coordinates of the centroid of a triangle whose vertices are

$A(x_1, y_1), B(x_2, y_2)$ and $C(x_3, y_3)$ are

$$\left[\frac{x_1 + x_2 + x_3}{3}, \frac{y_1 + y_2 + y_3}{3}\right]$$

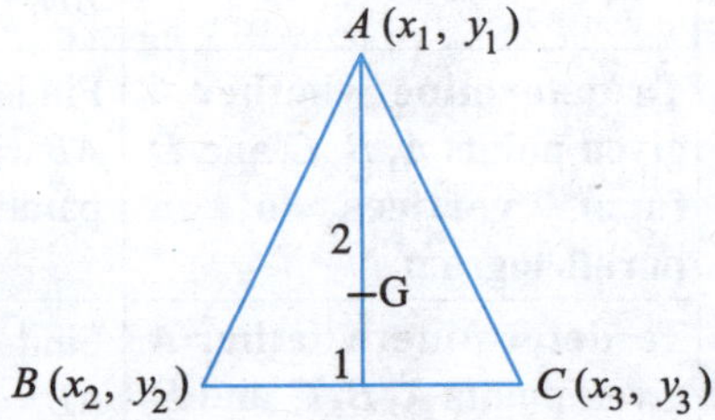

Applications of Section formula:

Type of problem	Solution
To find the ratio in which a given point divides the line segment joining two points $P(x_1, y_1)$ and $Q(x_2, y_2)$	Let the ratio be $k : 1$. Then, $x = \dfrac{kx_2 + x_1}{k+1}, y = \dfrac{ky_2 + y_1}{k+1}$
To find R the lengths of the medians of the triangle whose vertices are $A(x_1, y_1)$, $B(x_2, y_2)$ & $C(x_3, y_3)$ 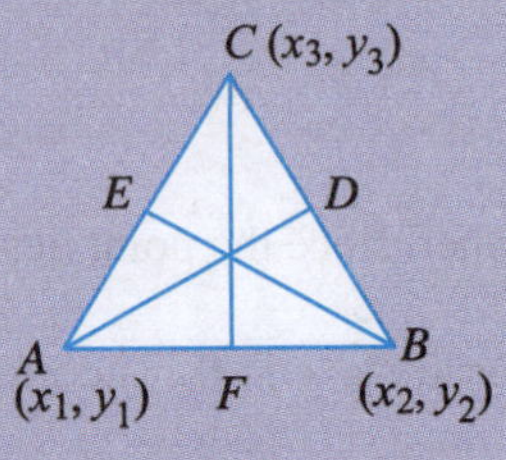	Let the medians be AD, BE and CF, where D, E and F are the mid-points of BC, AC and AB respectively. The coordinates of D are $\left(\dfrac{x_2 + x_3}{2}, \dfrac{y_2 + y_3}{2}\right)$ The coordinates of E are $\left(\dfrac{x_1 + x_3}{2}, \dfrac{y_1 + y_3}{2}\right)$ The coordinates of F are $\left(\dfrac{x_1 + x_2}{2}, \dfrac{y_1 + y_2}{2}\right)$ Then the lengths of the medians can be calculated by using the distance formula.

Given three vertices A, B and C of a parallelogram taken in order, to find the 4th vertex. 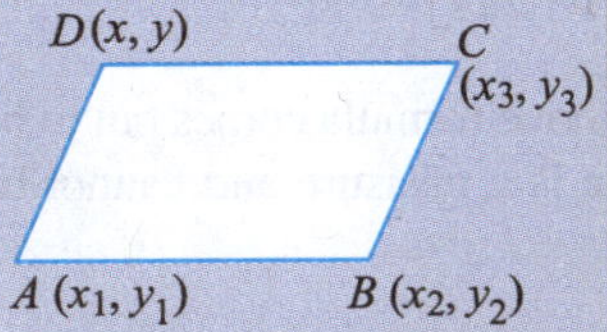	Let $D(x, y)$ be the 4th vertex. We know that the diagonals of a parallelogram bisect each other. Let the diagonals be AC and BD and let them intersect at O. Since the coordinates of A and C are known, the coordinates of the mid-point O can be found using the mid-point formula. The coordinates of mid-point of BD are also the same as O. Equating the two, x and y can be found.
To find the vertices of a triangle given the coordinates of the mid-points of the sides 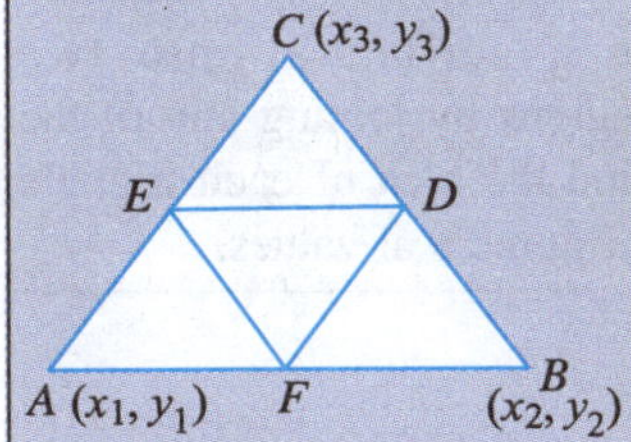	Let the coordinates of the vertices of the triangle be $A(x_1, y_1)$, $B(x_2, y_2)$ and $C(x_3, y_3)$. Let D, E and F be the mid-points of sides BC, AC and AB respectively. Then using the mid-point formula, The coordinates of D are $\left(\frac{x_2+x_3}{2}, \frac{y_2+y_3}{2}\right)$ The coordinates of E are $\left(\frac{x_1+x_3}{2}, \frac{y_1+y_3}{2}\right)$ The coordinates of F are $\left(\frac{x_1+x_2}{2}, \frac{y_1+y_2}{2}\right)$ Soling the equations, the vertices can be found.
To find the centriod of the triangle If three vertex of triangle is given 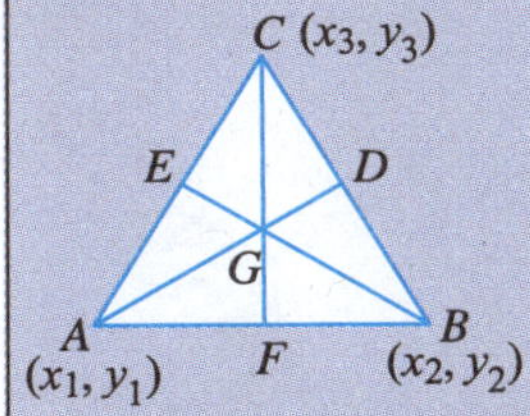	The coordinates of the centroid G of a triangle whose vertices are $A(x_1, y_1)$, $B(x_2, y_2)$ and $C(x_3, y_3)$ are given by $\left[\frac{x_1+x_2+x_3}{3}, \frac{y_1+y_2+y_3}{3}\right]$
To prove that the diagonals of a rectangle bisect each other and are equal 	Let the coordinates of the vertices of the rectangle be A (0, 0), B (a, 0), C (a, b) and D (0, b). Then the lengths of the diagonals AC and BD can be calculated using distance formula. Also, mid-point of AC = mid-point of BD. AC and BD, thus, bisect each other.

Area of a Triangle

Let ABC be a triangle whose vertices are $A\ (x_1, y_1)$, $B\ (x_2, y_2)$ and $C\ (x_3, y_3)$.The area of $\Delta\ ABC$ is the numerical value of the expression

$$\frac{1}{2}\left[x_1(y_2-y_3)+x_2(y_3-y_1)+x_3(y_1-y_2)\right].$$

Note: If the area as evaluated by using the above formula comes out to be negative, we shall take it as positive, since area is a measure and cannot be negative.

Applications of Area Formula:

Type of problem	Solution
To prove that three given points $A\ (x_1, y_1)$, $B\ (x_2, y_2)$ and $C\ (x_3, y_3)$ are collinear.	Find the area formed by the given three points. If area is 0, the three points are collinear.
To find the area of a quadrilateral whose vertices are given.	Divide the quadrilateral into two triangular regions by joining any of the diagonals.Find the area of each triangle and add their numerical values.

CHAPTER 8

TRIGONOMETRY

Introduction

The word **'trigonometry'** is derived from the Greek words **'tri'** (meaning three), **'gon'** (meaning sides) and **'metron'** (meaning measure). It is the study of relationships between the sides and angles of a triangle.

The trigonometric ratios of an acute angle in a right triangle express the relationship between the angle and the length of its sides. The trigonometric ratios of the angle *A* in right triangle *ABC* are defined as follows:

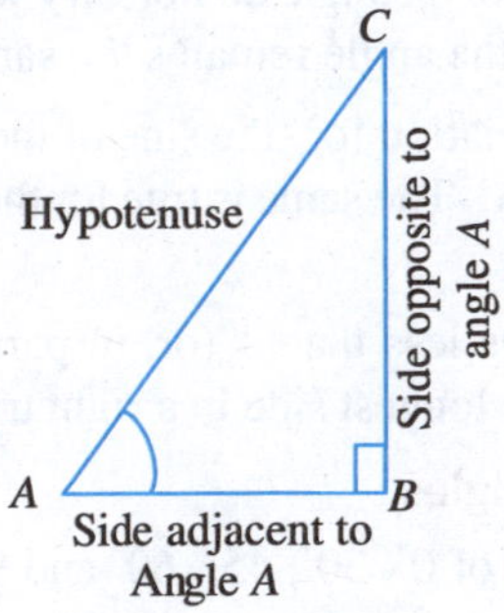

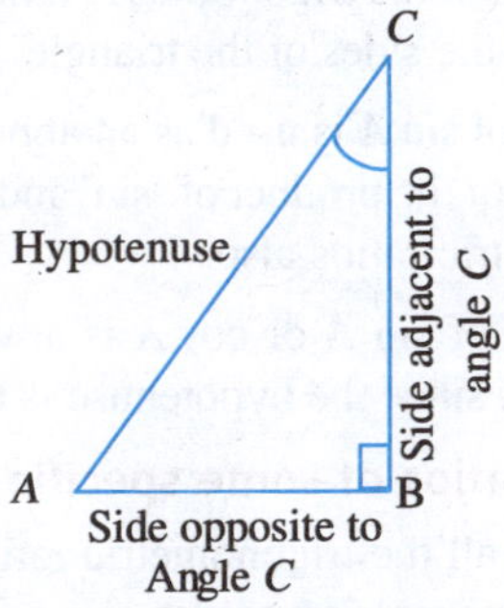

1. sine of $\angle A = \sin A = \dfrac{\text{side opposite to angle } A}{\text{hypotenuse}} = \dfrac{BC}{AC}$

2. cosine of $\angle A = \cos A = \dfrac{\text{side adjacent to angle } A}{\text{hypotenuse}} = \dfrac{AB}{AC}$

3. tangent of $\angle A = \tan A = \dfrac{\text{side opposite to angle } A}{\text{side adjacent to angle } A} = \dfrac{BC}{AB}$

4. cosecant of $\angle A = \text{cosec } A$

$$= \frac{1}{\text{sine of } \angle A} = \frac{\text{hypotenuse}}{\text{side opposite to angle } A} = \frac{AC}{BC}$$

5. secant of $\angle A = \sec A$

$$= \frac{1}{\text{cosine of } \angle A} = \frac{\text{hypotenuse}}{\text{side adjacent to angle } A} = \frac{AC}{AB}$$

6. cotangent of $\angle A = \cot A$

$$= \frac{1}{\text{tangent of } \angle A} = \frac{\text{side adjacent to angle } A}{\text{side opposite to angle } A} = \frac{AB}{BC}$$

Memory Tips

$$\frac{PBP}{HHB} = \frac{\text{Pandit Badri Prasad}}{\text{Har Har Bole}}, \text{Sona Chandi Tole}$$

$$\frac{P}{H} = \sin\theta \quad \text{or} \quad \text{cosec}\,\theta = \frac{H}{P}$$

$$\frac{B}{H} = \cos\theta \quad \text{or} \quad \sec\theta = \frac{H}{B}$$

$$\frac{P}{B} = \tan\theta \quad \text{or} \quad \cot\theta = \frac{B}{P}$$

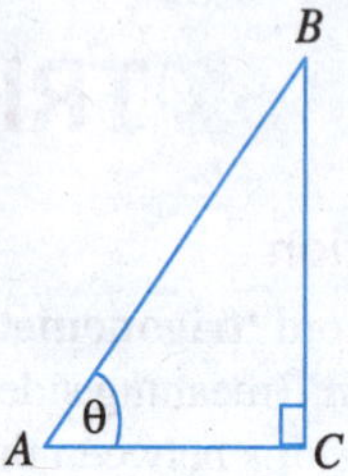

Sona $\rightarrow s \rightarrow \sin\theta$, Chandi $\rightarrow c \rightarrow \cos\theta$ and Tole $\rightarrow t \rightarrow \tan\theta$

Note:

1. The values of the trigonometric ratios of an angle do not vary with the lengths of the sides of the triangle, if the angle remains the same.
2. The symbol sin A is used as an abbreviation for 'the sine of the angle A' and is not the product of 'sin' and 'A'. The same is true for the other trigonometric ratios also.
3. The value of sin A or cos A is always less than 1 (or, in particular, equal to 1) since the hypotenuse is the longest side in a right triangle.

Trigonometric Ratios of some specific angles

The values of all the trigonometric ratios of 0°, 30°, 45°, 60° and 90° are given in the following table for ready reference:

Angle	0°	30°	45°	60°	90°
sin A	0	$\frac{1}{2}$	$\frac{1}{\sqrt{2}}$	$\frac{\sqrt{3}}{2}$	1
cos A	1	$\frac{\sqrt{3}}{2}$	$\frac{1}{\sqrt{2}}$	$\frac{1}{2}$	0
tan A	0	$\frac{1}{\sqrt{3}}$	1	$\sqrt{3}$	∞
cosec A	∞	2	$\sqrt{2}$	$\frac{2}{\sqrt{3}}$	1
sec A	1	$\frac{2}{\sqrt{3}}$	$\sqrt{2}$	2	∞
cot A	∞	$\sqrt{3}$	1	$\frac{1}{\sqrt{3}}$	0

Note ∞ = Not defined

Trigonometric ratios of complementary angles:

1. $\sin(90° - A) = \cos A$
2. $\cos(90° - A) = \sin A$
3. $\text{cosec}\,(90° - A) = \sec A$
4. $\sec(90° - A) = \text{cosec}\,A$
5. $\tan(90° - A) = \cot A$
6. $\cot(90° - A) = \tan A$

Complementary Angles

θ and 90°– θ are complementary angles, as their sum is $\theta + (90° - \theta) = 90°$

Ratio	Reciprocal ratio	Relationship
sin θ	cosec θ	$\sin\theta = \dfrac{1}{\text{cosec}\,\theta}$
cos θ	sec θ	$\cos\theta = \dfrac{1}{\sec\theta}$
tan θ	cot θ	$\tan\theta = \dfrac{1}{\cot\theta}$

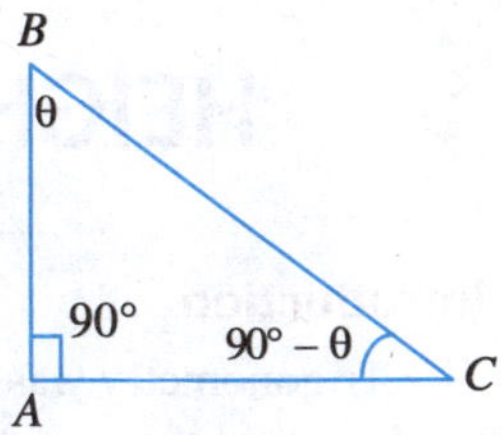

Trigonometric identities:

1. $\sin^2 A + \cos^2 A = 1$

   or, $\sin^2 A = 1 - \cos^2 A \quad \Rightarrow \quad \sin A = \sqrt{1-\cos^2 A}$

   Similarly, $\cos^2 A = 1 - \sin^2 A \quad \Rightarrow \quad \cos A = \sqrt{1-\sin^2 A}$

2. $\sec^2 A = 1 + \tan^2 A \quad \Rightarrow \quad \sec^2 A - \tan^2 A = 1$

   or, $\sec A = \sqrt{1+\tan^2 A}$ Similarly, $\tan^2 A = \sec^2 A - 1$

   or, $\tan A = \sqrt{\sec^2 A - 1}$

3. $\text{cosec}^2 A = 1 + \cot^2 A \qquad \text{cosec}^2 A - \cot^2 A = 1$

   or, $\text{cosec}\, A = \sqrt{1+\cot^2 A}$

   Similarly, $\cot^2 A = \text{cosec}^2 A - 1$ or, $\cot A = \sqrt{\text{cosec}^2 A - 1}$

4. $\tan\theta = \dfrac{\sin\theta}{\cos\theta}, \quad \cot\theta = \dfrac{\cos\theta}{\sin\theta}$

Note : A Regular Polygon :- A polygon is said to be regular when its all sides are of equal lengths and its all interior angles are of equal measures. If a regular polygon is of n sides, its each interior angle measures $\left[\left(\dfrac{n-2}{n}\right)\times 180\right]^\circ$.

If a regular polygon of n sides is inscribed in a circle, then it has each central angle of measure $\left(\dfrac{360°}{n}\right)$

CHAPTER 9

HEIGHTS AND DISTANCES

Introduction

Trigonometry was invented because its need arose in astronomy. It is also used in geography and in navigation. The knowledge of trigonometry is used to construct maps, determine the position of an island in relation to the longitudes and latitudes.

Line of Sight

The Line of sight is the line drawn from the eye of an observer to the point in the object viewed by the observer.

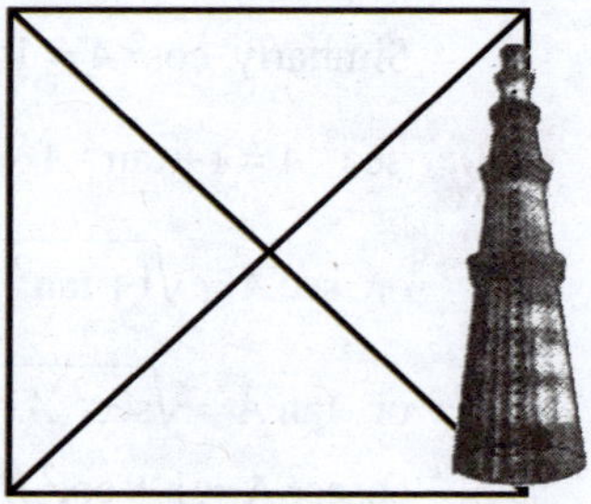

Angle of elevation

The angle formed by the line of sight and the horizontal line, when an observer sees an object situated in upward direction is called the angle of elevation.

Angle of depression

The angle formed by the line of sight and the horizontal line, when an observer sees an object situated in downward direction is called the angle of depression.

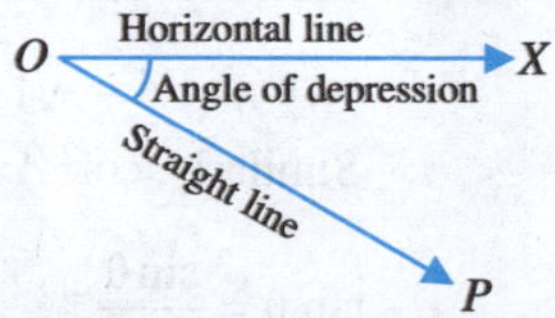

Key for Height and Distance

Key to solving problems on 'Height and Distance' is the ability to draw the right diagram on the basis of the conditions given in the problem. After that simple geometry and trigonometry knowledge will help in getting the required answer.

Concepts and Formulae

1. The angle of elevation of the top of a tower, standing on a horizontal plane, from a point A is α. After walking a distance 'd' towards the foot of the tower, let the angle of elevation is found to be β. Then height of the tower

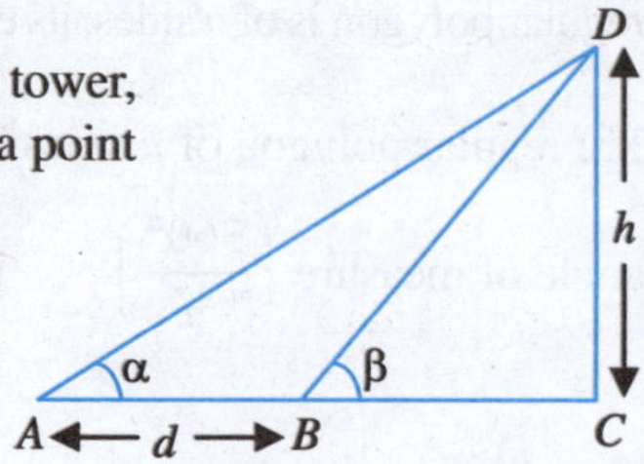

$$h = \frac{d \sin\beta \sin\alpha}{\sin(\beta - \alpha)} \text{ or } h = \frac{d}{\cot\alpha - \cot\beta}$$

2. If the points of observation A and B lie on either side of tower, then height of the tower

$$h = \frac{d \sin\beta \sin\alpha}{\sin(\alpha+\beta)} \text{ or } h = \frac{d}{\cot\alpha + \cot\beta}$$

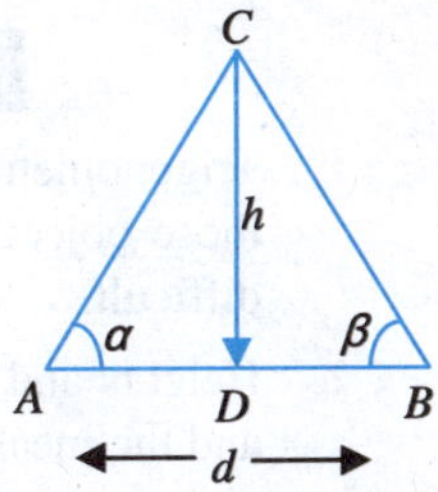

3. If angle of elevation of the top of a tower from the bottom and top of a building of height 'd' are β and α respectively, then height of the tower

$$h = \frac{d \sin\beta \cos\alpha}{\sin(\alpha-\beta)}$$

or $h = \dfrac{d \cot\alpha}{\cot\alpha - \cot\beta}$

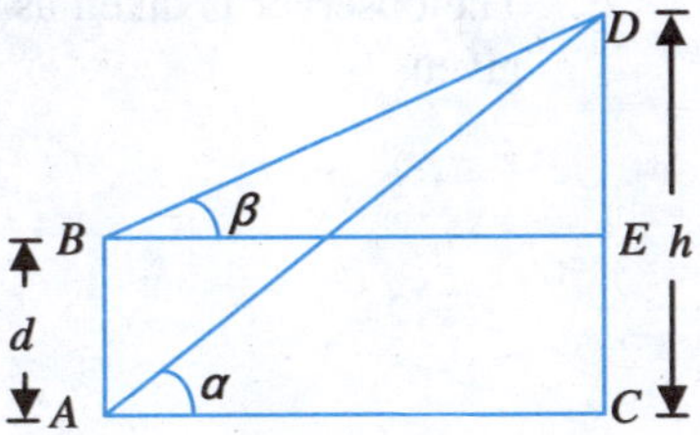

4. Let angle of elevation of a cloud from a height 'd' above the level of water in a lake is 'α' and the angle of depression of its image in the lake is 'β', then height of the cloud from the water level

$$h = \frac{d \sin(\beta+\alpha)}{\sin(\alpha-\beta)}$$

or $h = \dfrac{d(\tan\beta + \tan\alpha)}{\tan\beta - \tan\alpha}$ or $h = d\left[\dfrac{\cot\alpha + \cot\beta}{\cot\alpha - \cot\beta}\right]$

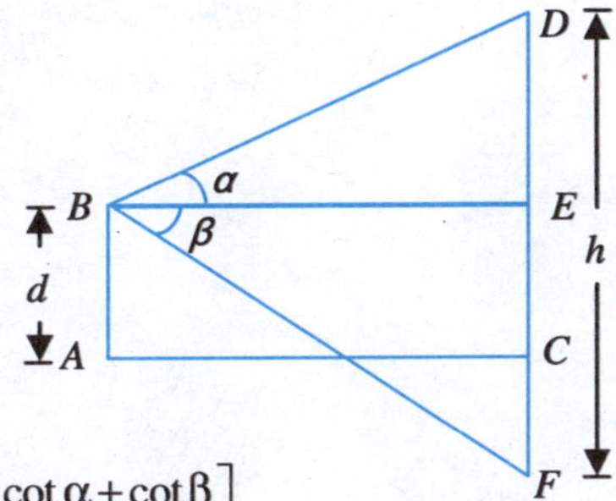

5. A balloon is observed simultaneously from the three points A, B, C on a straight road directly beneath it. The angular elevation at B is twice that at A and the angular elevation at C is thrice that at A. If $AB = a$ and $BC = b$, then height of the balloon in terms of a and b is

$$h = \frac{a}{2b}\sqrt{(3b-a)(a+b)}$$

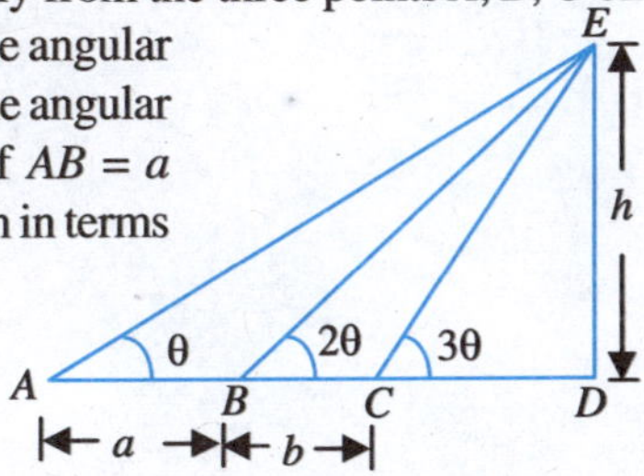

6. A flag staff stands on the top of a tower of height h. If tower and flag staff subtend equal angles at a distance 'd' from the foot of the tower, then height the flag staff is

$$h = \left[\frac{d^2 + h^2}{d^2 - h^2}\right]$$

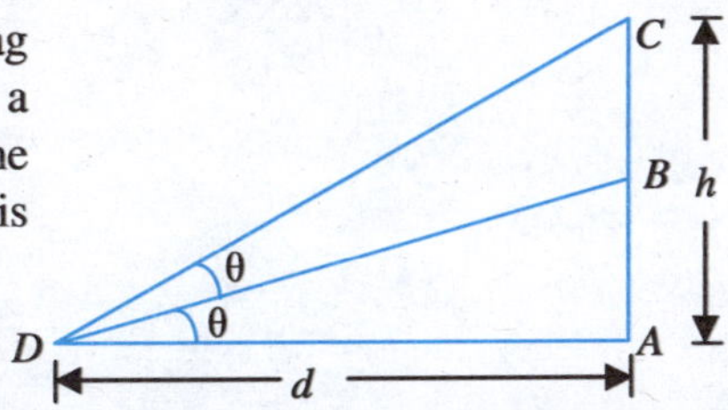

POINTS TO REMEMBER

1. Trigonometric ratios are used to determine the height and distance of those objects for which certain direct measurements of lengths are difficult.
2. Heights and distances may easily be determined if we know angles and the measure of a related length.
3. The observer is taken as a point unless the height of the observer is given.

CHAPTER 10

CIRCLES

Tangent to a circle

A tangent to a circle is a line that touches the circle at only one point. The tangent to a circle is a special case of the secant, when the two end points of its corresponding chord coincide. The common point of the tangent and the circle is called the point of contact and the tangent is said to touch the circle at the common point.

1. **Tangent:** A tangent is a line that touches a circle at only one point. The point at which the tangent touches the circle is known as the point of contact.

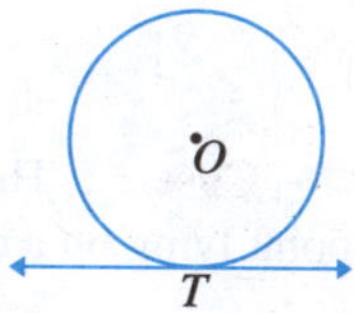

(*i*) A tangent to a circle is perpendicular to the radius through the point of contact. Given a circle $C(O, r)$ and a tangent AB to the circle at a point P, then $OP \perp AB$.

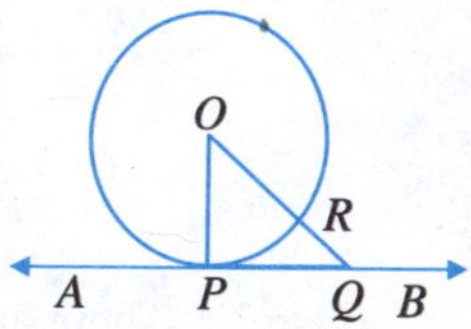

(*ii*) Conversely, a line through a point on a circle perpendicular to the radius through the point is the tangent to the circle at that point. Given a circle $C(O, r)$ of radius OP and a line APB perpendicular to OP. Then, AB is a tangent to the circle at P.

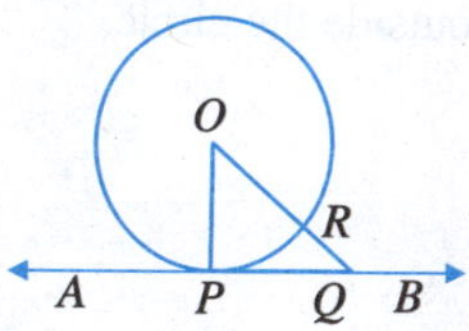

(*iii*) The lengths of the two tangents drawn from an external point to a circle are equal. AP and AQ are two tangents from a point A to a circle $C(O, r)$.

Then, $AP = AQ$.

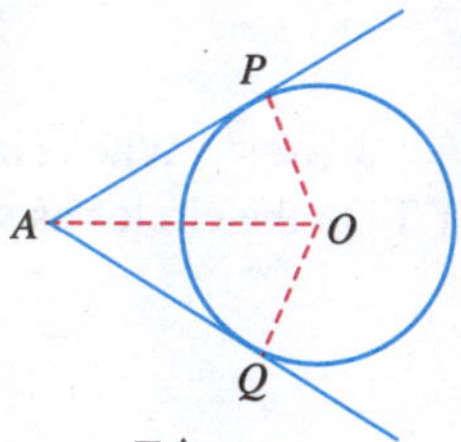

(*iv*) If two circles touch each other, the point of contact lies on a line joining their centres. Given two circles $C(O, r)$ and $C(O' s)$ touching each other at a point A.
Then the points O, O' and A are collinear.

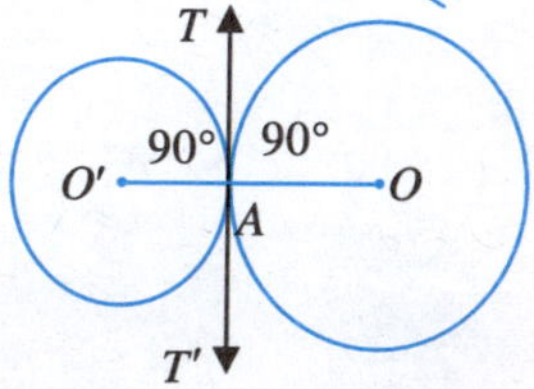

2. **Secant:** A secant is a line that intersects a circle at two distinct points.

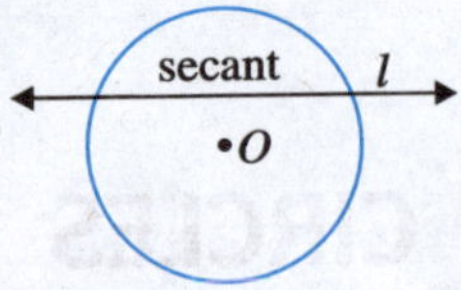

Circles and Common Tangents

Number of tangents from a point on a circle

Case 1: There is no tangent to a circle passing through a point lying inside the circle.

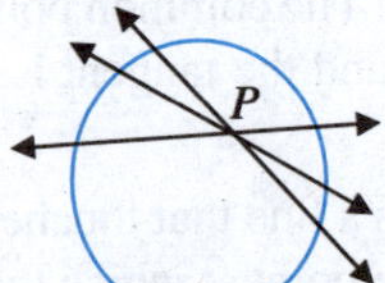

Case 2 : There is one and only one tangent to a circle passing through a point lying on a circle.

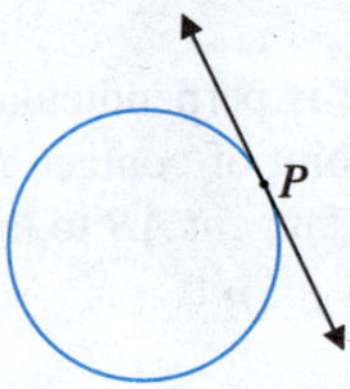

Case 3 : There are exactly two tangents to a circle through a point lying outside the circle.

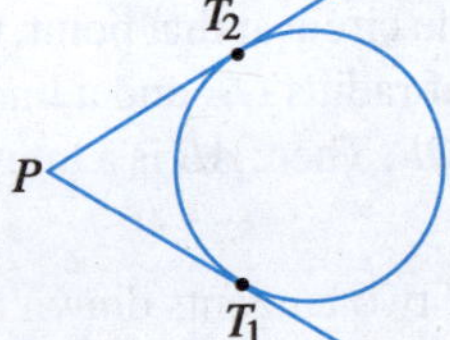

Case 4 : When circles touch internally. There is only one common tangent T T´ to the circles as shown in fig.

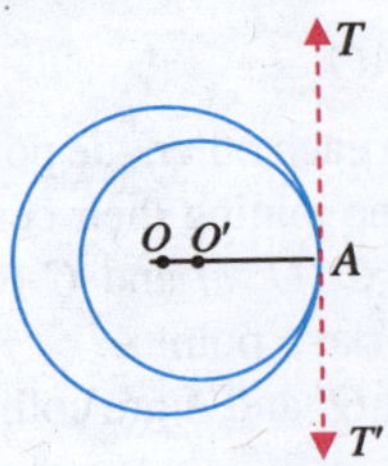

Memory Tips

S.No.	Position of two circles	Number of common tangents
1.	Two circles intersect at two distinct points	Two (2)
2.	Two circles touch externally	Three (3)
3.	One circle lies entirely outside the other	Four (4)
4.	One circle lies entirely inside the other	Zero (0)
5.	Two circles touch internally	One (1)

POINTS TO REMEMBER

1. The tangent at any point of a circle is perpendicular to the radius through the point of contact.
2. The lengths of tangents drawn from an external point to a circle are equal.
3. If two chords of a circle intersect inside or outside the circle, then the rectangle formed by the two parts of one chord is equal in area to the rectangle formed by the two parts of the other.
4. If *PAB* is a secant to a circle intersecting it at *A* and *B* and *PT* is a tangent, then $PA \times PB = PT^2$.
5. Two tangents drawn at the end points of a diameter of a circle are parallel.
6. The point of intersection of the direct common tangents and the centres of the circles are collinear, *i.e.*, *O*, *P* and *Q* be on the same line.
7. Tangents *TP* and *TQ* are drawn to a circle with centre *O* from an external point *T*, then $\angle PTQ = \angle OPQ$
8. Two parallel radii of a circle meet at a third tangent at *A* and *B*. Then *AB* subtends a right angle at the centre.
9. The length of a direct common tangent to two circles is $\sqrt{d^2-(r_1-r_2)^2}$ where *d* is the distance between the centres of the circles and r_1 and r_2 are the radii of given circles.
10. If all the sides of a quadrilateral touch a circle, then the sum of a pair of opposite sides is equal to the sum of the sides of the other pair.
11. If two chords of a circle intersect inside or outside the circle, the area of the rectangle formed by the segments of one chord is equal in area to the rectangle formed by the segments of the other.

CHAPTER 11

GEOMETRICAL CONSTRUCTIONS

Division of a Line Segment:

To divide a line segment in a given ratio.

Given a line segment AB, we want to divide it in the ratio $m : n$, where both m and n are positive integers. Let us take $m = 3$ and $n = 2$.

Steps of Construction :

1. Draw any ray AX, making an acute angle with AB.
2. Locate 5 $(= m + n)$ points A_1, A_2, A_3, A_4 and A_5 on AX so that $AA_1 = A_1A_2 = A_2A_3 = A_3A_4 = A_4A_5$.
3. Join BA_5.
4. Through the point A_3 $(m = 3)$, draw a line parallel to A_5B (by making an angle equal to $\angle AA_5B$) at A_3 intersecting AB at the point C (see Fig.). Then, $AC : CB = 3 : 2$.

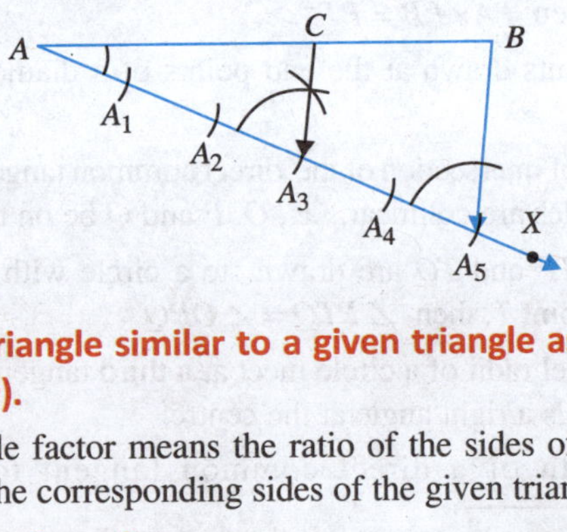

To construct a triangle similar to a given triangle as per given scale factor (say $m : n$).

Here, the scale factor means the ratio of the sides of the triangle to be constructed with the corresponding sides of the given triangle.

Steps of construction when $m < n$:

1. Draw any ray BX making an acute angle with BC on the side opposite to the vertex A.
2. Locate n (the greater of m and n in $m : n$) points B_1, B_2, B_3 and B_n on BX so that $BB_1 = B_1B_2 = B_2B_3 = B_{n-1}B_n$.
3. Join B_nC and draw a line through B_{n-1} parallel to B_nC to intersect BC at C'.

4. Draw a line through C' parallel to the line CA to intersect BA at A'

   Then, $\Delta A'BC'$ is the required triangle.

Steps of construction when $m > n$:

1. Draw any ray BX making an acute angle with BC on the side opposite to the vertex A.
2. Locate m (the greater of m and n in $m : n$) points B_1, B_2, B_3 and B_m on BX so that $BB_1 = B_1B_2 = B_2B_3 = B_{m-1}B_m$.
3. Join B_mC and draw a line through B_{m-1} parallel to B_mC to intersect BC at C'.
4. Draw a line through C' parallel to the line CA to intersect BA at A'

   Then, $\Delta A'BC'$ is the required triangle.

To construct the tangents to a circle from a point outside it.

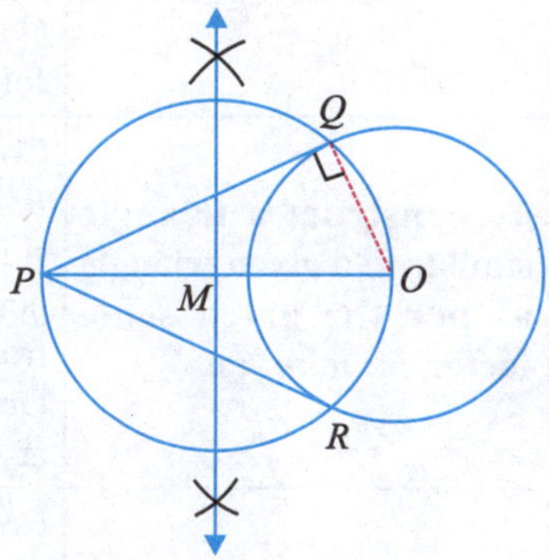

We are given a circle with centre O and a point P outside it. We have to construct the two tangents from P to the circle.

Steps of Construction:

1. Join PO and bisect it. Let M be the midpoint of PO.
2. Taking M as centre and MO as radius, draw a circle. Let it intersect the given circle at the points Q and R.
3. Join PQ and PR. Then PQ and PR are the required two tangents.

Important Concept

Type of construction	Steps of construction
Construction of a tangent when point of tangency lies on the circle and centre is given.	Draw a circle of given radius taking O as the centre. Take a point P on the circle. Join OP. Construct $\angle OPX = 90°$. Produce XP to Y. XPY is the required tangent.
Construction of a tangent when point of tangency lies on the circle and centre is not given.	Draw any chord PQ of the circle through the given point P. Take any point R on the major arc PQ and join PR and QR. Construct $\angle QPX = \angle PRQ$. PX is the required tangent at P to the circle.

Construction of a tangent when point of tangency is outside the circle and centre is given.	Join the centre O of the circle to the given external point P. Draw the right bisector of OP, intersecting OP at M.Taking M as the centre and MP as the radius, draw a circle to intersect the given circle at Q and Q'. Join PQ and PQ' to get the required tangents as PQ and PQ'.
Construction of a tangent when point of tangency is outside the circle and centre is not given.	Through the given external point P draw a secant PAB which intersects the circle at A and B.Bisect PB. Let M be the mid-point of PB.Taking M as centre and MP as radius, draw a semicircle.Draw a line perpendicular to PB through A which intersects the semicircle at C.Taking P as centre and PC as radius, draw arcs to intersect the given circle at two points, Q and R. Join PQ and PR to get the required tangents.
To construct a triangle similar to a given triangle as per the given scale factor, m: n, $m < n$	Construct the required triangle.From the vertex B, draw a ray BX at an acute angle on opposite side of A.Mark n equal arcs on BX. Let these points be X_1, X_2, X_3, ..., X_n.Join X_n to C and from X_m, draw a line X_mC' parallel to X_nC. Draw a line $C'A'$ parallel to CA intersecting BA at A'.$A'BC'$ is the required triangle.
To construct a triangle similar to a given triangle as per the given scale factor, $m : n$, $m > n$	Construct the required triangle.From the vertex B, draw a ray BX at an acute angle on opposite side of A.Mark m equal arcs on BX. Let these points be X_1, X_2, X_3, ..., X_m.Join X_n to C and from X_m, draw a line X_mC' parallel to X_nC. Draw a line $C'A'$ parallel to CA intersecting BA produced at A'.$A'BC'$ is the required triangle.
To construct a quadrilateral similar to a given quadrilateral as per the given scale factor, m : n	Draw a quadrilateral $ABCD$.Join BD and draw any ray BX inclined at an acute angle with BD. Starting from B, cut off n equal line segments BX_1, BX_2, .. , BX_n on BX. Join DX_n and draw a line segment X_mD' parallel to X_nD to intersect BD at D'.Draw a line $D'A'$ parallel to DA which intersects AB in A' and $D'C'$ parallel to DC which intersects BC at C'. $A'BC'D'$ is the required quadrilateral.

CHAPTER 12

AREAS RELATED TO CIRCLES

Perimeter of a circle

The distance covered by travelling once around a circle is called its perimeter, usually called its circumference. We know that the ratio of the circumference of a circle and its diameter is a constant, π. In other words,

$$\frac{\textbf{circumference}}{\textbf{diameter}} = \pi. \text{ **Or, circumference = } \pi \times \text{diameter.**}$$

Area of a circle

The area of a circle of radius 'r' is $A = \pi r^2$

Areas of Sector and Segment of a Circle

Consider a circle of radius r having its centre at O. The portion or part of the circular region enclosed by two radii and the corresponding arc is called a sector of the circle.

AOPB is called the minor sector and *OAQB* is called the major sector.

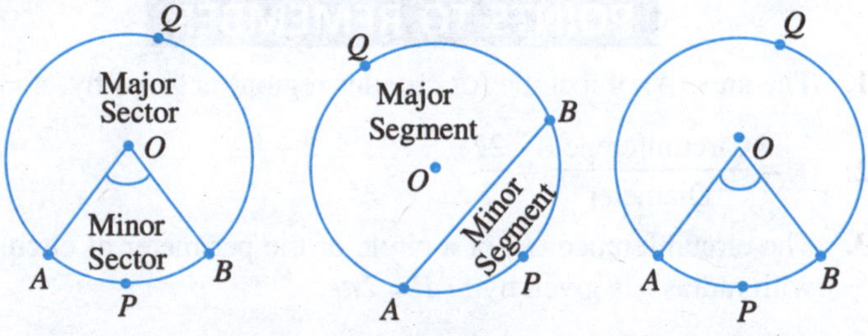

The portion or part of the circular region enclosed between a chord and the corresponding arc is called a segment of a circle. *APB* is called the **minor segment** and *AQB* is called the major segment.

Angle of the sector: The angle subtended by an arc at the centre is called the angle of the sector.

In the adjoining fig, $\angle AOB$ is called the angle of the sector.

Area of the sector of angle θ: The area of the sector of angle θ is given by $\frac{\theta}{360} \times \pi r^2$, where r is the radius of the circle and the angle of the sector in degrees.

Length of an arc of a sector of angle : The length of an arc of a sector of angle θ is given by $\frac{\theta}{360} \times 2\pi r$.

Area of segment: Area of segment *APB* = Area of the sector *OAPB* – Area of $\Delta\, OAB$

$$= \frac{\theta}{360} \times \pi r^2 - \text{Area of } \Delta\, OAB$$

Area of major sector *OAQB* = πr^2 - Area of the minor sector *OAPB*

Area of major segment *AQB* = πr^2 - Area of the minor segment *APB*

Distance moved by a wheel: Consider a wheel of radius *r*.

The distance moved by the wheel in one revolution = Circumference of the wheel.

Let the distance moved by the wheel in *n* revolutions $\frac{s}{n}$ be *s*. Then, the distance covered by the wheel in one revolution is , which is equal to the circumference of the wheel, .

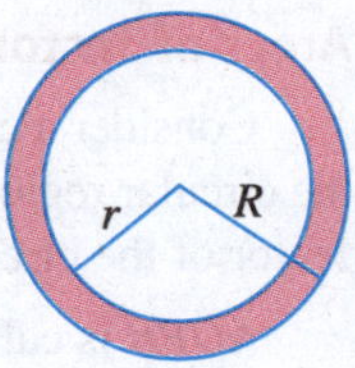

Area enclosed by two concentric circles: Let *R* and *r* be the radii of two concentric circles. Then, the area enclosed by the two circles is given by

$$\pi R^2 - \pi r^2 = \pi\left(R^2 - r^2\right) = \pi(R+r)(R-r)$$

POINTS TO REMEMBER

1. The area (*A*) of a circle (or circular region) is given by: $A = \pi r^2$.

2. $\pi = \frac{\text{Circumference}}{\text{Diameter}} = \frac{22}{7}$.

3. The circumference (*P*) of a circle or the perimeter of circular region with radius *r* is given by : $P = 2\pi r$

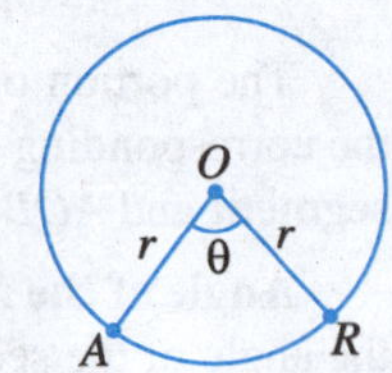

4. $\frac{\text{Area of sector of a circle}}{\text{Area of circle}} = \frac{\text{Sectorial angle } \theta°}{360°}$

   area of a sector of circle

   $= \frac{\theta°}{360°} \times \text{area of circle} = \frac{\theta}{360°}\pi r^2$

5. $\frac{\text{Arc } AB}{\text{Circumference of circle}} = \frac{\text{Sectorial angle } \theta°}{360°}$

   arc $AB = \frac{\theta}{360°} \times \text{Circumference of circle} = \frac{\theta}{360°}.2\pi r = \frac{\pi\theta r}{180^0}$

6. Perimeter of a sector of a circle = $\left(\frac{\pi\theta r}{180°}+2r\right)=\left(\frac{\pi\theta}{180°}+2\right)r$.

7. Area of semicircle = $\frac{1}{2}\pi r^2$

8. Perimeter of a semicircle = πr

9. Area of quadrant of a circle = $\frac{1}{4}\pi r^2$.

10. Perimeter of quadrant of a circle = $\left(\frac{\pi}{2}+2\right)r$ because a quadrant of circle is sector of the circle whose sectorial angle is 90°. Here r is the radius of the circle.

11. Area of regular hexagon

$= 6 \times$ area of equilateral ΔAOB

$= 6\times\frac{\sqrt{3}}{4}\times OA^2 = \frac{3\sqrt{3}}{2}\times(\text{side})^2$ sq. units.

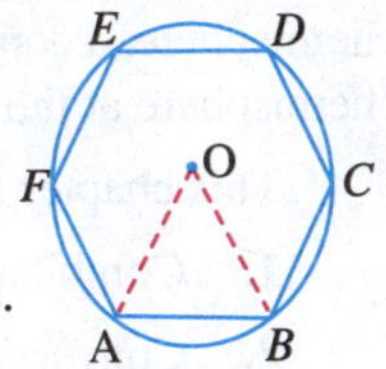

12. Area of the minor segment (ABM)

$=\left[\frac{\pi r^2\theta}{360°}-\frac{1}{2}r^2\sin\theta\right]$

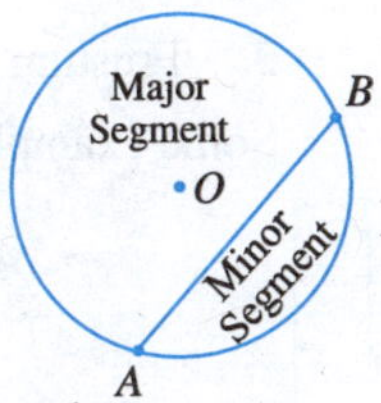

13. In radius of a circle (r) = $\frac{\Delta}{s}$

where r = radius of a circle inscribed in a given triangle

Δ = area of the given triangle

s = half perimeter of the given triangle

or $s=\frac{a+b+c}{2}$ for all a, b, c are the sides of a given triangle.

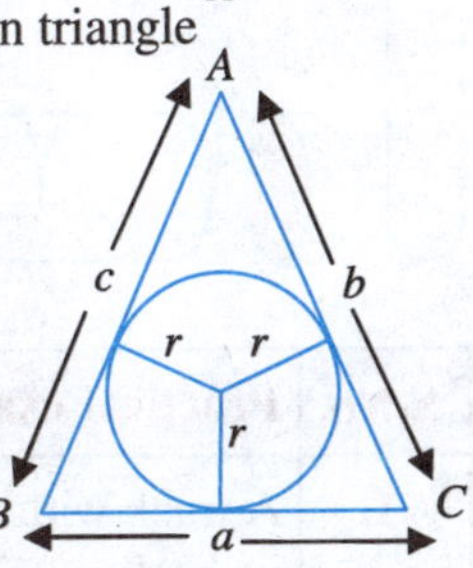

14. Circum radius (R) = $\frac{abc}{4\Delta}$ where

R = radius of circumcircle described about a given triangle with sides a, b, c.

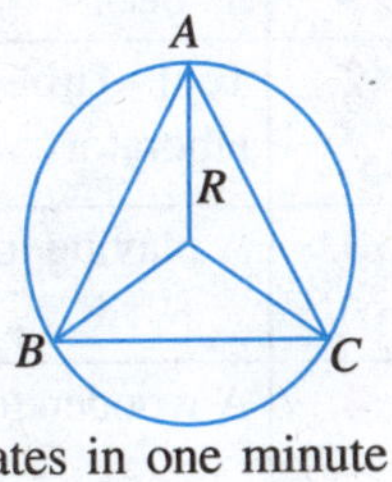

15. The angle through which the minute-hand rotates in one minute is

$\frac{360°}{60°}=6°$

CHAPTER 13

VOLUME AND SURFACE AREAS

Volume and Surface Areas

In our day-to-day life, we come across a large number of objects made up of combinations of two or more of the basic solids such as a cylinder and a hemisphere, a cone and a hemisphere, a cylinder with a cone at one end and a hemisphere at the other end.

This chapter is basically divided into three parts which are:

1. Combination of Solids
2. Conversion of Solids
3. Frustum of a Right Circular Cone

Some examples of combination of solids:

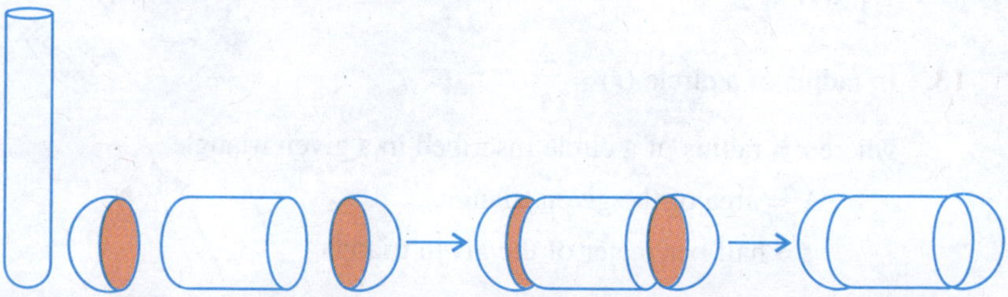

S.No.	Practical example	Explanation
1.	A truck with a cylinder fitted on its back	It is made up of a cylinder with two hemispheres as its ends
2.	Test Tube used in science laboratory	It is made up of a cylinder with a hemisphere as its one end
3.	A playing top (*lattu*)	It is made up of a cone with a hemisphere as its one end
4.	A wooden toy rocket	It is made up of a cylinder mounted by a cone
5.	A medicine capsule	It is made up of a cylinder with two hemispheres as its ends

The important formulae to find the curved surface area, total surface area and volume of solids are given below :

The following symbols will be used for all cases unless stated otherwise :

l = length of a cuboid, b = breadth of a cuboid, h = height of a cuboid

a = side/edge of a cube

r = radius of base of a cone and cylinder

r = radius of a sphere and hemisphere

l = slant height of a right circular cone

h = vertical height of a cone/height of a right circular cylinder

Remember: Volume of a solid = Area of the Base X height

Frustum of a cone:

If a cone is cut with a plane parallel to its base and the cone that is formed on one side of that plane is removed, the part that is left on the other side of the plane is called a frustum of the cone.

Let h be the height, l is the slant height and r_1 and r_2 are the radii of the ends ($r_1 > r_2$) of the frustum of a cone. Then we can find the volume, the curved surface area and the total surface area by using the formulae given below:

Volume of the frustum of a cone	$\frac{1}{3}\pi h\left(r_1^2 + r_2^2 + r_1 r_2\right)$
Curved surface area of the frustum of a cone	$\pi(r_1 + r_2)l$, where $l = \sqrt{h^2 + (r_1 - r_2)^2}$
Total surface area of the frustum of the cone	$\pi(r_1 + r_2)l + \pi r_1^2 + \pi r_2^2$, where $l = \sqrt{h^2 + (r_1 - r_2)^2}$

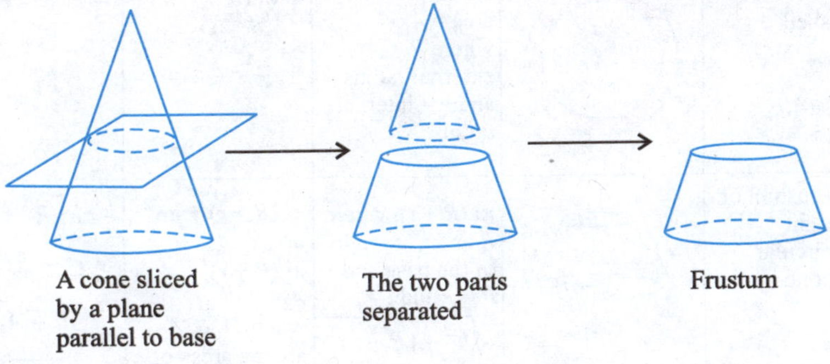

Solid	Figure	Lateral/Curved Surface Area	Total surface Area	Volume
Cuboid	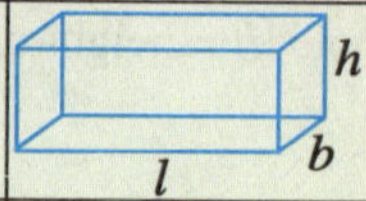	$2 \times (l + b) \times h$	$2 \times (lb + bh + lh)$	$l \times b \times h$
Cube	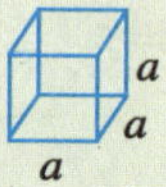	$4 \times a^2$	$6 \times a^2$	a^3
Right Circular cylinder	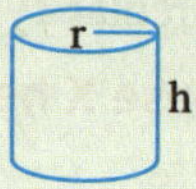	$2\pi rh$	$2\pi r^2 + 2\pi rh$	$\pi r^2 h$
Right Circular Cone	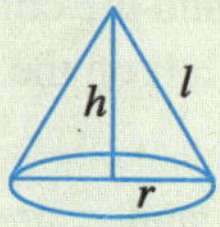	πrl, $l = \sqrt{r^2 + h^2}$ Where l = slant hight	$\pi rl + \pi r^2$	$\frac{1}{3}\pi r^2 h$
Sphere	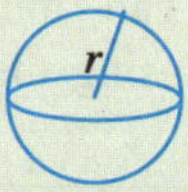	$4\pi r^2$	$4\pi r^2$	$\frac{4}{3}\pi r^3$
Hemisphere	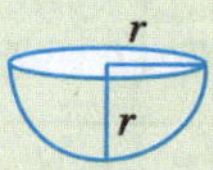	$2\pi r^2$	$3\pi r^2$	$\frac{2}{3}\pi r^3$
Hollow cylinder	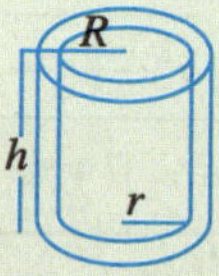	$2\pi (R + r)h$, where R = external radius and r = internal radius of base	$2\pi (R + r)h + 2\pi (R^2 - r^2)$	$\pi (R^2 - r^2) h$
Spherical shell	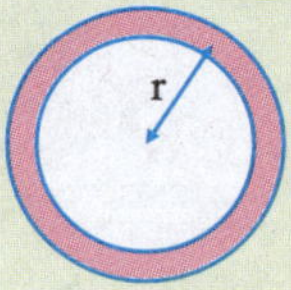	Outer surface area = $4\pi r^2$, where R = external radius and r = internal radius	$4\pi (R^2 - r^2)$	$\frac{4}{3}\pi(R^3 - r^3)$
Frustum of right circular cone	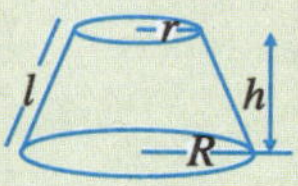	$\pi l (R + r)$, where R and r are radii of the base and $R > r$ and $l = \sqrt{h^2 + (R - r)^2}$	$\pi l (R + r) + \pi R^2$ or $\pi l (R + r), + A_1 + A_2$ where A_1 & A_2 are the areas of the base	$\frac{1}{3}\pi h\left[R^2 + r^2 + Rr\right]$ or $\frac{h}{3}\left[A_1 + A_2 + \sqrt{A_1 + A_2}\right]$

Combination of solids

TSA of the new solid = CSA of 1st solid + CSA of 2nd solid + CSA of 3rd solid +...

We shall find the surface area of solids made up of a combination of two basic solids. We shall also see how to calculate their volumes. It may be noted that in calculating the surface area, we do not add the surface areas of the two constituents, because some part of the surface area disappear in the process of joining them. However, this will not be the case when we calculate the volume. The volume of the solid formed by joining two basic solids will actually be the sum of the volumes of the constituents.

Conversions of Solids

Conversion of solid	Formulae
A metallic sphere or ball of radius '*R*' melted and recast into n smaller spherical balls of radius '*r*'.	$\frac{4}{3}\pi R^3 = n \times \frac{4}{3}\pi r^3$ or $n = \frac{R^3}{r^3}$
A metallic sphere or ball of radius '*R*' melted and recast into a long wire of radius '*r*' and length '*h*'.	$\frac{4}{3}\pi R^3 = \pi r^2 h$
A metallic spherical shell of external radius 'r_2' and internal radius 'r_1' is melted and recast into *n* smaller spherical balls of radius '*r*'.	$\frac{4}{3}\pi(r_2^3 - r_1^3) = n \times \frac{4}{3}\pi r^3$
A metallic cone of radius '*R*' and height '*h*' is melted and recast into *n* balls each of radius '*r*'.	$\frac{1}{3}\pi R^2 h = n \times \frac{4}{3}\pi r^3$
A metallic spherical shell of external radius 'r_2' and internal radius 'r_1' is melted and recast into a solid circular cylinder of height '*h*' and radius '*r*'.	$\frac{4}{3}\pi(r_2^3 - r_1^3) = \pi r^2 h$
A metal ball of radius '*R*' is melted and recast into 3 spherical balls of radii 'r_1', 'r_2' and 'r_3'.	$\frac{4}{3}\pi R^3 = \frac{4}{3}\pi r_1^3 + \frac{4}{3}\pi r_2^3 + \frac{4}{3}\pi r_3^3$
A spherical ball of radius '*R*' is dropped into a cylindrical vessel of base radius '*r*' partly filled with water.	Let the rise in level of water by '*h*'. Then, $\frac{4}{3}\pi R^3 = \pi r^2 h$

Water from a hemispherical shell of external radius r_2 and internal radius r_1 is transferred to n bottles of base radius 'r' and height 'h'.	$\frac{2}{3}\pi(r_2^3 - r_1^3) = n \times \pi r^2 h$
Largest sphere carved out of a cube of side 'a'.	Diameter of sphere, $2r$ = side/edge of the cube. $r = a/2$
Largest right circular cone that can be carved out of a cube of edge 'a'.	Diameter of base of cone, $2r$ = side/ edge of the cube. $r = a/2$
***n* circular plates or coins of radius 'r' and thickness 'h' are placed one above the other to form a solid right circular cylinder.**	Height of cylinder = nh Volume of 'n' plates= $n \times \pi r^2 h$ Total Surface area = $2\pi r(r + nh)$

CHAPTER 14

STATISTICS

Introduction

We shall discuss numerical representatives of grouped data, also called measures of central tendencies, namely, mean, median and mode. We shall also discuss the concept of cumulative frequency, the cumulative frequency distribution and how to draw cumulative frequency curves, called ogives.

Mean of Grouped Data

The mean (or average) of observations is the sum of the values of all the observations divided by the total number of observations.

Let $x-_1, x_2, x_3, \ldots, x_n$ be the observations having frequencies $f_1, f_2, f_3, \ldots, f_n$ respectively. The mean of the data is given by

$$\bar{x} = \frac{f_1x_1 + f_2x_2 + \ldots + f_nx_n}{f_1 + f_2 + \ldots + f_n} = \frac{\sum_{i=1}^{n} f_ix_i}{\sum_{i=1}^{n} f_i}$$

In the case of a grouped frequency distribution table, for each class-interval, we require a point which would serve as the representative of the whole class. The mid-point (or its class mark) of each class can be chosen to represent the observations falling in the class as it is assumed that the frequency of each class-interval is centered around its mid-point. That is,

$$\textbf{Class Mark} = \frac{\textbf{Upper class limit + Lower class limit}}{\textbf{2}}$$

1. Arithmetic Mean

There are three methods of finding the mean of given data:

Methods of Finding Means

Direct Method

$$\bar{x} = \frac{\sum f_ix_i}{\sum f_i}$$

Shortcut Method

$$\bar{x} = A + \frac{\sum f_id_i}{\sum f_i}$$ where

A = Assumed Mean

$d_i = x_i - A$

Step-Deviation Method

$$\bar{x} = A + h \times \frac{\sum f_iu_i}{\sum f_i}$$

Where $u_i = \dfrac{x_i - A}{h}$

2. Direct method of finding Mean

Consider ungrouped data $x_1, x_2, x_3, .., x_n$ occurring with frequencies $f_1, f_2, f_3, ..., f_n$ respectively. Then the mean is given by:

$$\overline{x} = \frac{f_1x_1 + f_2x_2 + f_3x_3 + ... + f_nx_n}{f_1 + f_2 + f_3 + ... + f_n} = \frac{\sum f_ix_i}{\sum f_i} = \frac{\sum f_ix_i}{N}, \text{where } N = \sum f_i$$

In case of grouped data, first find $x_i = \frac{(\text{Upper limit} + \text{lower limit})}{2}$.

Multiply f_i with corresponding x_i to get f_ix_i.

Add all f_ix_i to get $\sum f_ix_i$.

Divide by N to get $\overline{x}$.

MERITS AND DEMERITS OF MEAN

Merits of Mean

- It is rigidly defined.
- It is easy to calculate and simple to follow.
- It is based on all the observations.
- It is determined for almost every kind of data.
- It is finite and not indefinite. $\sum f_id_i$
- It is readily put to algebraic treatment.
- It is least affected by fluctuations of sampling.

Demerits of Mean

- The arithmetic mean is highly affected by extreme values.
- It cannot average the ratios and percentages properly.
- It is not an appropriate average for highly skewed distributions.
- It cannot be computed accurately if any item is missing.
- The mean sometimes does not coincide with any of the observed value.

3. Short-cut or Assumed Mean method for finding Mean

First assume any value of x_i as the mean, A. Calculate the deviations, d_i, of each x_i from the assumed mean using $d_i = x_i - A$.

Multiply f_i with corresponding d_i to get f_id_i. Add all f_id_i to get .

Substitute in the formula $\overline{x} = A + \frac{\sum f_id_i}{\sum f_i}$ to calculate the mean.

Relation between $\overline{d}$ and $\overline{x}$: $\overline{d} = \overline{x} - a$, *i.e.*, $\overline{x} = a + \frac{\sum f_id_i}{\sum f_i}$.

4. Step-Deviation Method for calculating Mean

First assume any value of x_i as the mean, A. Calculate the deviations, d_i, of each x_i from the assumed mean using $d_i = x_i - A$. Divide deviations by h to get u_i as $u_i = \dfrac{x_i - A}{h}$.

Multiply f_i with corresponding u_i to get f_iu_i. Add all f_iu_i to get $\sum f_iu_i$.

Substitute in the formula $\overline{x} = A + h \times \dfrac{\sum f_iu_i}{\sum f_i}$ to calculate the mean.

Relation between $\overline{u}$ and $\overline{x}$: $\overline{x} = a + h\overline{u} = a + h\left(\dfrac{\sum f_iu_i}{\sum f_i}\right)$:

Note:

1. The step deviation method will be convenient to apply if all the d_i's have a common factor.
2. The assumed mean method and the step-deviation method are just simplified forms of the direct method.
3. If x_i and f_i are sufficiently small, then the direct method is an appropriate choice.
4. If x_i and f_i are numerically large numbers, then we can go for the assumed mean method or step-deviation method.
5. If the class-sizes are unequal, and x_i are large numerically, we can still apply the step-deviation method by taking h to be a suitable divisor of all the d_i's.

Mode of Grouped Data

A mode is that value among the observations which occurs most often, that is, the value of the observation having the maximum frequency.

In a grouped frequency distribution, we can only locate a class with the maximum frequency, called the modal class. The mode is a value inside the modal class, and is given by the formula :

$$\text{Mode} = l + \left[\frac{f_1 - f_0}{2f_1 - f_0 - f_2}\right] \times h, \text{ where}$$

l = lower limit of the modal class,

h = size of the class interval,

f_1 = frequency of the modal class,

f_0 = frequency of the class preceding the modal class,

f_2 = frequency of the class succeeding the modal class.

Uses Of Mode

Mode is the average to be used to find the ideal size, *e.g.*, in business forecasting, in manufacturing of ready-made garments, shoes, *etc.*

Merits of Mode

- It can be easily understood and is easy to calculate.
- It is not affected by extreme values.
- It can be found by inspection in some cases.
- It can be measured even if open-end classes.
- It can be represented graphically.

Demerits of Mode

- It is ill-defined. It is not always possible to find a clearly defined mode.
- It is not based upon all the observations.
- It is not capable of further mathematical treatment. It is often indeterminate. It is affected to a greater extent by fluctuations of sampling.

Median of Grouped Data

The median is a measure of central tendency which gives the value of the middle-most observation in the data. We first find the value inside a class that divides the whole distribution into two halves, after making a cumulative frequency distribution. To find this class, called the median class, we find the cumulative frequency of all the classes and $\frac{n}{2}$. We next locate the class whose cumulative frequency is greater than (and nearest to) $\frac{n}{2}$. This is the median class. We then use the following formula for calculating the median:

$$\text{Median} = l + \left[\frac{\frac{n}{2} - cf}{f}\right] \times h,$$

Where l = lower limit of the median class,

h = size of the class interval,

n = number of observations,

cf = cumulative frequency of class preceding the median class,

f_1 = frequency of the modal class,

f_0 = frequency of the class preceding the modal class,

f_2 = frequency of the class succeeding the modal class.

Merits and Demerits of Median

Merits of Median

- It is easily understood.
- It is not affected by extreme values.
- It can be found even if some items are not known.
- It can be determined by inspection is some cases.
- It is useful when the data cannot be measured quantitatively.

Demerits of Median

- It requires the arraying of data which is very difficult when the number of items is very large.
- It is not suitable for algebraic calculations.
- In case of even number of total frequencies, it cannot be determined exactly.
- It is not useful when extreme items are to be given importance.
- It may not be the representative of the series when the distribution of items is irregular, *i.e.*, items vary greatly in magnitude.

Remarks :

1. There is a empirical relationship between the three measures of central tendency :

   3 Median = Mode + 2 Mean
2. The median of grouped data with unequal class sizes can also be calculated.

Graphical representation of Cumulative frequency Distribution

To represent the data in the table graphically, we mark the upper limits of the class intervals on the horizontal axis (*x*-axis) and their corresponding cumulative frequencies on the vertical axis (*y*-axis), choosing a convenient scale. The scale may not be the same on both the axes.

Consider the table:

Marks	Number of students
0 – 10	5
10 – 20	3
20 – 30	4
30 – 40	3
40 – 50	3
50 – 60	4
60 – 70	7
70 – 80	9
80 – 90	7
90 – 100	8

We can construct the cumulative frequency distribution table as given below :

Marks	Number of students (*f*)	Cumulative frequency (*cf*)
0 – 10	5	5
10 – 20	3	8
20 – 30	4	12
30 – 40	3	15
40 – 50	3	18
50 – 60	4	22
60 – 70	7	29
70 – 80	9	38
80 – 90	7	45
90 – 100	8	53

We now plot the points corresponding to the ordered pairs given by (upper limit, corresponding cumulative frequency), *i.e.*, (10, 5), (20, 8), (30, 12), (40, 15), (50, 18), (60, 22), (70, 29), (80, 38), (90, 45), (100, 53) on a graph paper and join them by a free hand smooth curve. The curve we get is called a **cumulative frequency curve**, or an **ogive** (of the less than type).

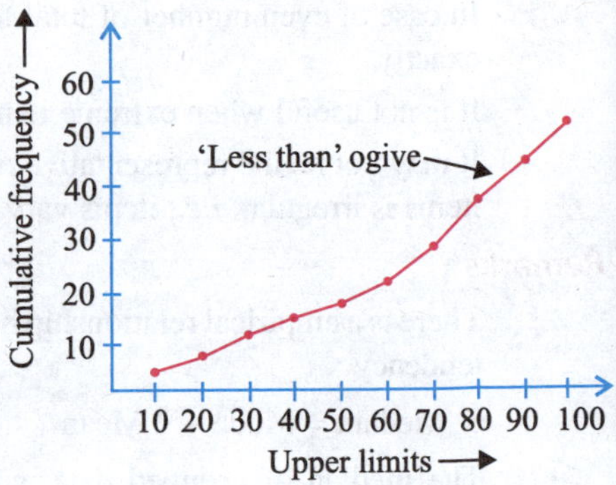

To represent 'the more than type' graphically, we plot the lower limits on the *x*-axis and the corresponding cumulative frequencies on the *y*-axis. Then we plot the points (lower limit, corresponding cumulative frequency), *i.e.*, (0, 53), (10, 48), (20, 45), (30, 41), (40, 38), (50, 35), (60, 31), (70, 24), (80, 15), (90, 8), on a graph paper, and join them by a free hand smooth curve.

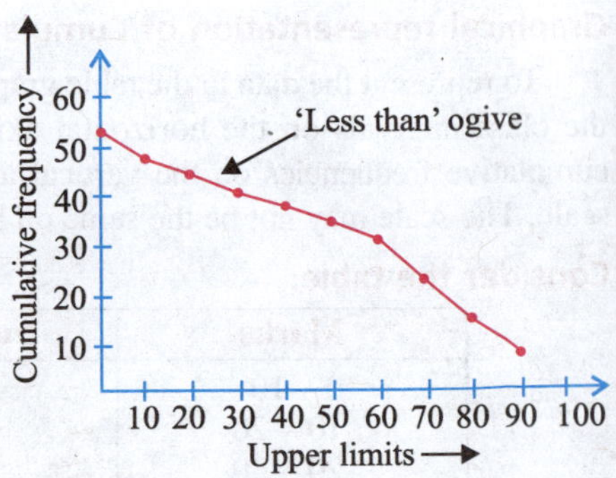

The curve we get is a cumulative frequency curve, or an ogive (of the more than type).

Note: For drawing ogives, it should be ensured that the class intervals are continuous.

To determine the Median from an ogive

One way is to locate $\frac{n}{2} = \frac{53}{2} = 26.5$ on the y-axis as given in fig. From this point, draw a line parallel to the x-axis cutting the curve at a point. From this point, draw a perpendicular to the x-axis. The point of intersection of this perpendicular with the x-axis determines the median of the data as shown in the fig below.

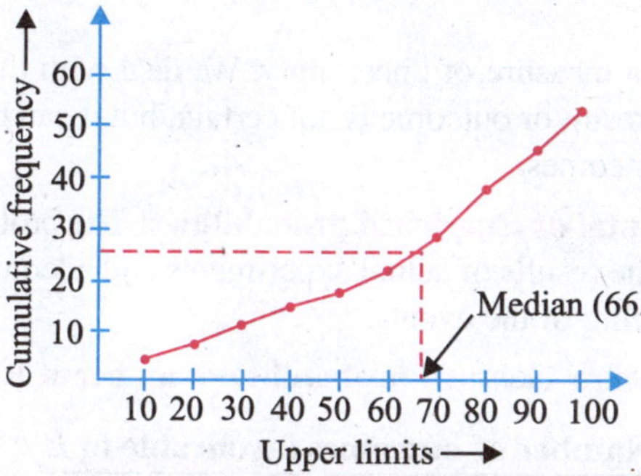

Another way of obtaining the median is the following

Draw both ogives (*i.e.*, of the less than type and of the more than type) on the same axis. The two ogives will intersect each other at a point. From this point, if we draw a perpendicular on the x-axis, the point at which it cuts the x-axis gives us the median as shown in fig below:

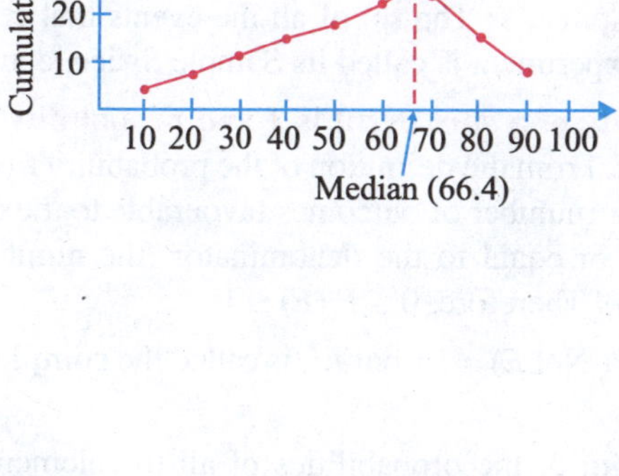

CHAPTER 15

PROBABILITY

Probability

Probability is a measure of uncertainty. We deal with those situations in which a particular result or outcome is not certain, but it can be any one of the several possible outcomes.

(*a*) **Experimental or Empirical probabilities**: The probabilities that are based on the results of actual experiments and adequate recordings of the happening of the events.

(*b*) **Theoretical or classical probability of an event E:**

$$P(E) = \frac{\textbf{Number of outcomes favourable to } E}{\textbf{Total Number of possible outcomes}}$$

(*c*) **Event:** The outcome of an experiment is called an event.

(*d*) **Elementary event:** An event having only one outcome of the experiment is called an elementary event. The sum of the probabilities of all the elementary events of an experiment is 1.

(*e*) **Equally likely events:** If we can reasonably assume that each outcome of an elementary experiment is as likely to occur as the other, We refer to this by saying that the outcomes head and tail, are equally likely. For example, the equally likely outcomes of throwing a die are 1, 2, 3, 4, 5 and 6.

(*f*) **Sample Space, *S*:** The set of all the events that could be associated with an experiment is called its Sample Space, denoted by *S*.

(*g*) **Probability of a sure event is 1 and probability of an impossible event is 0.** From the definition of the probability $P(E)$, we see that the numerator (number of outcomes favourable to the event E) is always less than or equal to the denominator (the number of all possible outcomes). Therefore, $0 \leq P(E) \leq 1$

(*h*) $P(E) + P(\text{Not } E) = 1$ ['not E', is called the **complement** of the event E.]

Note: The sum of the probabilities of all the elementary events of an experiment is 1.

POINTS TO REMEMBER

1. An event for an experiment is the collection of some outcomes of the experiment.
2. The probability of an event A is given by
$$P(A) = \frac{\text{Number of favourable outcome } (A)}{\text{Total number of possible outcomes } (S)}.$$
3. The probability of an event lies between 0 and 1.
4. The sum of all probabilities is 1, *i.e.*, $p(S) = 1$.
5. The probability of an event is never negative.
6. $P(A) + P(\text{not } A) = 1$
7. $P(\phi \text{ or impossible event}) = 0$.
8. If A and B are two mutually exclusively events, then $P(A \text{ or } B) = P(A) + P(B)$
9. If A and B are two mutually exclusively events, then $P(A \text{ and } B) = \text{ only } \phi$.
10. If a die is thrown n times, then the total number of outcomes are 6^n.
11. If two events have the same probability, these are said to be equally likely events.
12. The face cards in a pack of 52 cards are : 4 Jack, 4 Queen and 4 Kings *i.e.*, total number of face cards = 4 + 4 + 4 = 12.
13. If odds in favour of an event A are $m : n$, then $P(A) = \frac{m}{m+n}$.
14. If odds against A are $m : n$, then $P(A) = \frac{n}{m+n}$.
15. The experiment or empirical probability of an event is based on what has actually happened while the theoretical probability of the event attempts to predict what happens on the basis of certain assumptions. As the number of trials in an experiment, go on increasing, we may expect the experimental and theoretical probabilities to be nearly the same.
16. The set of all possible outflows of an experiment is called sample space and denoted by S.
17. If an experiment (Condition under identical consumptions) can result in two or more outcomes, it is called random experiment.
18. The process of conducting the experiment is called trial, whereas, the outcomes are called events.
19. An action or operation resulting in a well defined outcome is called an experiment.

Important Facts

Coin. On tossing a coin, there are two possibilities, either head may come up or tail may come up.

Die. A die is a well balanced cube with its six faces marked with numbers (dots) from 1 to 6, one number on one face. The pural of die is dice.

Cards. A pack of cards consists of four suits (**Spades ♠ clubs ♣ Hearts ♥ Diamonds ♦**) each suits consists of 13 cards, Queen and Jack or Knave. Colour of Spades and Clubs is black and that of Hearts and Diamons is red and 12 face cards in a normal pack of 4 suits, and total red cards are 26 and total black cards are 26.

Spades

Clubs

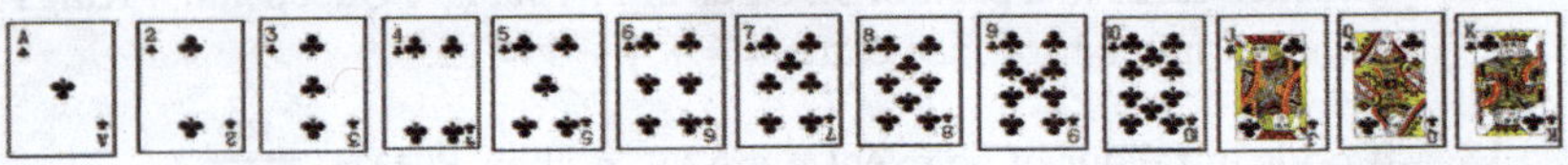

Hearts

Diamonds